NATHANIEL G. MOORE

Let's Pretend
We Never Met

LET'S PRETEND WE NEVER MET

Nathaniel G. Moore

Pedlar Press | Toronto

ACKNOWLEDGEMENTS
The publisher wishes to thank the Canada Council for the Arts and the Ontario Arts Council for their generous support of our publishing program.

LIBRARY AND ARCHIVES CANADA CATALOGUING IN PUBLICATION

Moore, Nathaniel G

  Let's pretend we never met / Nathaniel G. Moore. -- 1st ed.

Poems.

ISBN 978-1-897141-15-1

1. Catullus, Gaius Valerius--Poetry. I. Title.

PS8626.O595L482007   C811'.6   C2006-906928-X

First Edition

EDITED FOR THE PRESS Emily Schultz
COVER ART J.T. Winik
DESIGN Zab Design & Typography, Winnipeg

Printed in Canada

THE CANADA COUNCIL FOR THE ARTS SINCE 1957 | LE CONSEIL DES ARTS DU CANADA DEPUIS 1957

ONTARIO ARTS COUNCIL CONSEIL DES ARTS DE L'ONTARIO

For my brother Jeffrey, for all time, hail and farewell!

Being a man means living in nothingness.
Kathy Acker

TABLE OF CONTENTS

I. FRESH FROM THE COUGHING

Once I destroyed a man's idea of himself to have him.
Frank O'Hara

Introducing the Catullus[1] Gene

TWELVE YEARS ON, Catullus was a poet on whom I had no intention of giving up. He was someone I didn't particularly want to lose to another. By any means necessary I would be his and he would be mine. That's the thread of this storyline. So when I finally met up with his literary agent in late 2005 to discuss a new project, I felt like things were going to work out between us. The meeting was legendary, conducted at The Chelsea Room on Dundas Street West. The whisky sours, poured in front of low watt bulb cleavage, were anointed with spearmint, which partially cocooned the ice, creating an addictive residue. I reviewed all the letters I'd sent Catullus over the years. They were neatly tied up in a red silk scarf. Harvey Mandolini, Catullus's agent, showed me photographs of him on a ski trip, as well as some at his office. In one, Catullus was petting a black goat. "He sneezed on Catullus," Harvey recalled. "Catullus was terrified for months."

Next to him on the table were several letters Catullus had written to me but never mailed. I told Harvey about the project, and his eyes lit up. When I revealed the plan, which involved moving the bawdy bard into a house with some of his old friends, Harvey explained how as of late Catullus really "needed to interact with others," and how it seemed as if the poet were "in a real rut."

[1] Gaius Valerius Catullus was born in or near Verona in 84 BC to a family of considerable wealth and connections— his father was a friend of Julius Caesar. He was well educated and encouraged by his brother to write poetry. At the age of twenty-two, he moved to Rome and enjoyed all that high society had to offer.

It could be said that Catullus devoted his life to eroticizing pain rather than exorcising it. Have I read too deeply into his romantic crime-scene after-gashes? Perhaps. Upon hearing I was into Catullus, my grandfather wrote me in 1997: "And what is your interest in Catullus? I read his poetry in 1932 and thought little of it."

IDENTIDEM means *again and again*, and is found in Catullus's landmark piece in which he reveals a secret and married lover, Clodia Metelli, as Lesbia. (*Carmen LI*) In this word (*identidem*) I hear the word *tandem*, *identity* and of course *dent*. I also hear the word *identical*, as in identical acts: I *feel* this again and again, I *see* this happening again and again. I picture someone saying softly 'I *dented him*.' This takes my breath away. An obsessed congregation of one, talking in tongues. Perhaps two tongues. In Catullus's work, duality is a theme, the voice simultaneously loving and hating, expressing remorse and detachment, curiosity and apathy, without commitment to remain in either field, without commitment to an absolute.

It has been crucial that Catullus relive his own set of poetic circumstances and that I observe the rituals and symptoms of his disorder firsthand. This is the only way to prove that gene and syndrome exist. Furthermore it proves these symptoms are being passed on through the Y *Chromosome*. His original poems are land mines and sign posts for this quest, a set of realistic triggers to fray his heart strings. Seeing Rufus and Juventius was not strong enough an edifice to bring Catullus out of his [alleged] rut and back into the cruel but productive art of self-discovery and or destruction.

I talked to Harvey, discussed Lesbia (Clodia Metelli).

"Any chance she'd come to the house, for an interview or something?"

Harvey shook his head immediately. "Sorry kid, that's where

things are going to end. She has papers her lawyer and she drew up a few years back, making her not public domain. Catullus of course is a bit more desperate. You won't be allowed to use her likeness without her permission."

After three months culling prearranged romantic back-stories, time-released text messages and teary-eyed responses to accusations, I finished the outline for the experiment with a fictional little sister "Mahelly." (In truth there were four sisters, all named Clodia, which Catullus would know about.) Once cast, the willing Mahelly character seemed ready to play out her role in the experiment. Another month passed, I got a call from Harvey: Catullus is anxious to start.

"Does he know what year it is?" I ask Harvey.

"No, not really," Harvey said.

I told him things would not be ready for a few months and asked him to be patient.

I made some calls to publishers in Toronto to see if they'd ever published posthumous writing, would they be interested in publishing the dead. The responses were curious.

"I would like to see manuscripts from dead folks. To see if they've changed and modernized themselves in any way," said one publisher. Another said, "The reason we've never published posthumous writing is that we've never had any submissions. But an added detriment is this—certain funding bodies (Ontario Book Publishing Tax Credit, I think, for one) only fund books by living authors." Added another, "If somebody pulls a Lazarus? Depends on the writer. The new work would have to do something for me." And further still, on the chance of publishing a favourite writer's work after death, one publisher beamed, "Should one of our favourite poets return from the grave, we would probably want new stuff. Assuming she or he died in an interesting way and could write about that. But if they get all maudlin and sentimental, well, there's no additional room for that in CanLit. As long as it isn't light-at-the-end-of-the-tunnel crap, I think it might be more fun to publish posthumously written verse."

Carmen (the name of Catullus's manuscript) *II* and *III* rely on sparrow imagery for their emotional spine. Using a confluence of envy and cherish, Catullus writes about Lesbia's pet bird in an overtly sensual way. *III* mourns the bird's death while the prequel suggests a phallic projection or symbolic crossover. For these reasons I had to find a house with a history of sparrows, not just a couple of them, but a real sparrow problem, a house lodged in a heavy sparrow zone.

In March 2006 I received both fax and phone instructions from Lesbia/Clodia's lawyer, requesting that I send him an outline of the project, with all my notes and any taped interviews attached. I comply. He says he'll get back to me later that week, but he never calls.

By the summer of 2006 I secured a house and contacted Juventius, who was willing to help out. We painted the house, cleaned the kitchen counters, the windowsills. Each little crevice was hit up with double-knotted cloth wipes soaked in bleach and sterilization elixirs. Dust bunnies were snared, gardens pruned, recycling boxes ordered, carpets vacuumed, scented candles and potpourri scattered on end tables and bathroom nooks. With Catullus in place for a late fall 2006 stay, I arranged for Juventius and Rufus to move in beforehand. We decorated the living room in warm earth tones, with a focus on red and brown. We hung saffron on several walls and up the staircase. The royal treatment. The colour of love and blood. I am to live in the basement, undetected.

Rufus was the wildcard and I knew he wouldn't stick it out unless properly enticed. At first he just watched Canadian Parliament on television and read the newspaper in his room.

When Mahelly showed up for rehearsal, wading into the scene with a sort of lecherous sincerity, her mouth full of hairpins, eyelashes trafficking excess mascara, her thick hair piled and twisted high, Rufus's eyes bore through her. He showed not the slightest trace of self-consciousness. Catullus was now focused and ready for the project.

Perhaps Catullus's most complex work was *Carmen LXIII*, the Attis poem. In it Catullus deals with a strained duality of narcissism and extreme masochism. Attis, fresh from castration over failed love, runs howling, insane, into the forest. Catullus's use of the Attis legend expresses his own desire for escape, while demonstrating that pain is frightening. "Let all your rage be quite far from my home: provoke other men; make other men zealous!"

For his bit part, wayward lover Juventius hammed it up considerably and was a pleasure to work with. Tall, fit and humorous, clean-shaven, his green eyes punctuated by a dark laugh that dragged out into a long sexy hum. He often nodded his head in self-amusement, up to his elbows in dish soap or laundry. No one was allowed to leave the house without testing one of his new health shakes. Everyone loved Juventius. Every day in the kitchen wearing a bright yellow duck apron, usually sporting some type of sweatband with matching wristbands. He loved dragging Catullus to art shows, craft sales, even bake sales. Catullus tried to find ways to get out of the invitations.

"No reason you should miss this one," Juventius would say sweetly. Catullus knew no pain could come out of these activities and would dismiss Juventius's invites with a scowl and a wave of his hand.

Hidden within a Canadian poetry manuscript is a romantic battle plan where the Catullus Syndrome™ and Gene™ are proved once and for all. It is a theory that the obsessed becomes, at some stage, disenfranchised. He discovers other forms of eroticism beyond the object of his obsession (usually younger, or a close friend of the obsessed) and the timorous lovers spend several poems, chapters, weeks or months waffling between shame, distrust, regret and apathy. In the final analysis the obsessed will succumb to the final phrasing of *Carmen VIII* and "become stone" from the digestion of some pretty nasty pain variables. A pain variable is a condition or situation realized in disturbing hot flashes within the cracks of the psyche. Examples of pain variables include: text messages that read "I'm alone now, call me"; condom wrappers in bed; late night hang-ups; scratch marks. As for my own work, a continuous fascination with the maintenance of self-destruction is realized several times, in slow motion low budget masochism. These poems are still warm from the abject interactions from which they were born.

Jean-Paul Sartre once wrote of Genet, "Not all would be narcissist." Where's the drama in that? Therapeutic, neurotic, neutered, necrophilic, it's Catullus and me at our very best, and it's up next.

Dusk calms the motor. A clump of light brown feathers rolls off the windshield. Catullus and his agent are parked in front of a small bungalow. It's a cold October evening; red splits through the clouds with a hint of milky rain just beyond the rooftops. A capful of cough syrup jiggles as Catullus downs it. His agent nods supportively, taking off his driving gloves, turning his body sideways to face both Catullus and the house. He leans in and wipes a bit of magenta syrup from the side of the poet's mouth.

"See, not so bad."

"I am to go inside?"

"It's a really great project. Some of your friends are already there. They'll tell you about it."

"Like who tells?"

"Juventius, for one, and Rufus."

"Rufus?"

"Yes, Rufus."

"That guy, I do not feel like that guy."

"And also, there is Mahelly."

"Who do you say?"

"Mahelly, she's Clodia's younger sister."

"I do not very remember the name."

"She's supposed to be really cute."

"Are you sure that?"

"Yes."

"When you be here back?"

"I'll meet up with you later on in the book."

"What you just please say?"

"Next week sometime."

Curfew the Dead

*In Catullus's Rome, a pathetic fire-fighting system aimed toward
inaccuracy and third-storey flame with impotent hand pumps, or waited
circus-like with vinegar-drenched bedsheets for suicide jumpers; the most
valuable member of the rescue team was the good doctor.*

His toga soiled in unconfirmed stains roams,
mischievously tumbles, I add bleach to the cycle

Remember the coffin, how it glided despite
the stone-seeded road, describing death

to make-believe reporters who did skateboard tricks
with clipboards

Spastic streetlights sponged up our pimples
moths along our gums,

drunk from the humid, faith-eaten air—
God, what were you thinking?

Sleep is entertainment for those whose minds
have government

Curfew the dead, Catullus and I sew the earth
With lacerations, howling and proud,

parts of Roman culture pasted thoroughly
over my aggravated lampshade;

I reach for the switch, poorly painted and full of texture
hear moaning alleys, the crumbling market

colourful conquering, hooded alley shadows
consulting the tones of a pale civilian

Moon-tipped ink runs across barracks into the showers,
rusted locks, museum hair combed nightly by unionized guards

all tenderly watched through faceless security cameras,
the gutter tumbling by the seamstress shop

I have on light blue flannel antique pyjamas
that during the day dry in the congested sunlight

The lampshade full of his fingerprints, I clean it often
the storm outside begins, shadows lean

He walks into my room, the ancient earth holds his family,
holds me away from his body like a knife blade humming

He wore a pair of sandals on the ferry but in my backyard
I study the dust on his face mixing in with the garden salad,

harvest his rodent fingers, brush the leaves of lettuce
He watches them, wet green hems

At night my damp voice stains his phone, he washes
the receiver before putting it down

The naked heart showered, chunks of water break,
come down, root me out, make me invisible

before him. Sand in my stretched eye, a souvenir of
Catullus, torso and all; embroiled, plunged,

the wet heckler of fleshy union with a two-legged
smile. The patent is somewhere on a bookshelf

From the bathroom
Catullus talks in bilingual banters

Flesh tombs in a trunk, tucked into midnight drawers,
his fingers full of rings dent the lampshade.

No. 2

1. Throwing Nuts to the Slaves

starlings and house sparrows are non-native birds more aggres-
sive by nature and present year round taking over birdhouses,
natural nesting cavities used by woodpeckers or municipally
funded migratory songbirds including bluebirds or provincially
appointed chickadees

2. Slave Wage Buffet

fresh from the coughing, my body sewn minimally within then
released from cotton-vest garrison garnished with first name,
embossed tacky badge, I pluck cruel roadkill all afternoon, as
feather-flesh shifts itself to death. I crawl to its side, a

cowardly knight with broom/trash can lid dragging the dead back
to the villa, oven preheats, autopsy begins under the tweezered
sky; clumps of feathers neatly stuffed under the sink in ugly
discarded hairball asteroid

flesh remains to do the job: some paprika, cumin, cinnamon,
garlic, lemon, ribbed Tabasco sauce the minor bird, glaze it,
gelling it sizzlesmear on Teflon skin

meal ready, lights temperamental; wind chokes
                                candles flicker like death-
sentence storms, sink mood

                     Catullus comments on size,
meal, still dripping, our foul mouths cool under atmosphere's
emotional discourse

3. Discussion: The Meal Plan

"Why is our bird so small?"
"Do you have a job yet?"
"No"
"Shovel snow"
"In May?"
"Excuses are cheap"
"Explain the size we eat"
"With your empty salary we can't eat bigger game"

No. 2

Dear gone Sparrow, dearest of my girl's, whom she is accustomed to stroke,
whom she is accustomed to squeeze in her lap, for whom she lends her index finger
and provokes sharp bites, watched hop melodic with large planet drool eyes—
preheat the oven, cool your lips, it's another teasing fit
for this delicious pricey wife,

who slums it
with peasant crumpet
dripping on posh lips
gulps wads of lowlife

O scam and love me,
become
bird-thin, blow away

Fork through chest
Fork through chest
We dine on what
We dine on what
she loved best

"Why read poetry and suck a pain magnet
when you can eat lush seafood on a yacht
and never wear a watch again?"

"I hope you blow away, candlelike destroyer
If only I were able to play with you yourself, and

lighten the sad carousel that churns your mental
amphitheatre, you miss the bird too much
but it's right here, eat up, let your pet flutter
in intestinal finality."

The Thief's Journalism

(W)here to
begin?

We dictate the mood at the auction
where the object is stiff, displayed, ready,
knowing his fate, cleverly sealed in manila
snakeskinism or *snakism* amidst

are we in the crowd bidding or onstage
pushing toward the open mouths?

I graffiti the parking lot
in his verbs,
cranial x-rays,
statuesque remains,
spurts of DNA,
testimonials from living scholars, plus
handfuls of false molars
spreading like seed below my hand.

In the parking lot
hailing a cab
driver pretends to ignore
muffled panting
muffled panting.
At home privacy is drawn
I undo the envelope's vain
concealment,
the corduroy increases
along the banister, he rips at
my pants with curiosity.

My hands however—
a subconscious reconstruction of:
an uninsured past
blessed with extra auction bits.

Envelope:

meticulous invoices for other auction items on the block,
an IOU for 1000 socks, hand-labelled according to days of the
     week and usage,
plus—

"arrowhead dental floss" (25 bids)
"mint chipped teeth decadence" (32 bids)
"harpoon tart tea set" (125 bids)
"nurse-mouth soother" (190 bids)
"shark in wolf's clothing bankruptcy set" (2 bids)
"sex clotting decoder ring with asthma bath salts" (47 bids).

Bits fall after sneezing,
fall from the parchment
as the rust plunges
memorable, anchor deep,
in the pit of my cranky stomach,

I bite the sulphur
I tongue the coma

morbid pebbles
wake up and repeat the chorus

In sweet fortress, I share a tender runt of fish,
discover his alibis; the word *hookerstreak*

in window advertisements
while mannequins are looted in the market.

As I read, the sun immigrates,
igniting a clothesline in the process,
cuts my beta pupil
causing correction fluid
to spill everywhere,

which stings
under astute adoration, emulation
mistranslation, not dead yet
here I am, dirty, still no richer
the jingle, *Little is known.*

Catullus, the hemisphere is quoting you,
one heart attack at a time—

Gaius Valerius Catullus, whose name stands not lower than
third on the roll of Roman poets, was born in Verona 84 BC.
Son of a wealthy Veronese gentlemen and friend of Julius
Caesar, he moved tranquil from Verona to Rome about 62 BC.

At twenty-two, Catullus met Clodia, a married woman of
power. His unhappiness was complete when his brother died
in Asia. Notwithstanding, quarrelled and made friends with
Cicero. Enjoyed the best society, in all senses, of Rome.

Among his friends and contemporaries were C. Licinius
Calvus and M. Caelius Rufus, the latter of whom became rival
and enemy

(enemy, perhaps too narrow a word, but meant in a biological
warfare sense due to purposeful and artful placement and
manipulation of Rufus's lower extremities, and a powerful
finishing move. Rufus and Clodia arched a liaison, known
in some napkin gossip circles as deceptive un-contraceptive
lunging, O Rufus appropriated his mess ransacking the
sentimental party dress).

Three and only three independent witnesses to the full
text, all derived from a lost archetype (probably late twelfth
century) known to have been at Verona in the early 1400s and
hence conventionally referred to as V:

a society predicated on moments of attractive performance
can only collapse, vanity spits back into finely lubricated
frivolity.

Fabricate the rhyming scheme,
milk its tawdry apathy,

astonished, like the performance Romankind aims to
describe, things evanescent and unstable, scolded approaches
the life of passion, art, sensual domestic poisoning
necrophilic massage becomes too much of a message,
in this case virtually inextricable from the artist's intent,

never physical, space vacuumed up into selfish necessity; a
professed non-desire to verbalize hostility or actuality when
all that is needed is honest recruitment of normalcy of which
I am incapable.

By the early twentieth century, Catullus had become a full-blown romantic, in both Symons and Yeats we find in him a passionate lover scornful of the limits of bourgeois society:

L-----² says she'd
rather marry me
than anyone, though
Jupiter himself
came asking, or
so she says, but
what one tells their
lover in cloaked
desire should be
written out on air
or running water
illegible install a
hostile sprinkler
system   rot love
apoplectic.

force jewellery down
pipes as plumber
cracks his jaw thuds
on rhinestone sink,
soak his fuzzy dice
in the acid rain
of this   eternal
tantrum.

you are nothing, I think, that cannot be invented through
heightened masturbatory   detachment
within the prolific con   of creativity.

2 Clodia Metelli, wife of Quintus M. Celer, poetess, upper-class beauty, whom
Cicero called "Ox-eyes," was a controversial and powerful woman, accused of poi-
soning her husband. She had an affair with Catullus and would later have an affair
with Catullus's friend Rufus. Catullus hid Clodia's identity within the pseud-
onym "Lesbia," which he appropriated from Sappho's Island of Lesbos. Catullus
also chose "Les-b-ia" for its syllabic similarity to Clo-d-ia.

No. 4

Kimitaka Hiraoka was born in Tokyo,
the son of a government official. Later
he changed his name to Yukio Mishima.
The name Yukio can loosely be translated
as "man who chronicles reason." Mishima
was raised mainly by his paternal grandmother,
who hardly allowed the boy out of her sight.

During World War II, Mishima was excused
from military service, but he served in a factory.
This plagued Mishima throughout his life—
surviving shamefully when so many others
had been killed.

Thomas Chatterton was born in Bristol
on November 20, 1752, and is generally
regarded as the first Romantic poet in
English. He invented Thomas Rowley,
a fifteenth century monk, and wrote poetry
and published it on his behalf.

So many illusions here, look at how
they all connect, amputate edges
in this jigsaw piece, bend the form:

Clodia into Lesbia
Kimitaka into Yukio
Chatterton into Rowley.

Each carefully constructed
to ensure the creative integrity
would survive. Like Hallowe'en,

less temporary, a century-long
day worthy of its white chalk.

Gaius? Gaius? Gaius? Seriously listen
as cough syrup magenta curdles
on the parchment,
these g's torment:

(germinate glycerin germaphobe
gramophone grenade growl groin
gelignite girdle giddy growth spurt)

motion, bobbing whimpering applause;
is this the act convincingly deliberate
open-mouthed love left in the sun
a wet-cock fit, lazy hand through
Juventius's toxic blond hair—marigolds
yellowing desperate, as the unwell sturgeon
moves awkward in unlit lake, gardening
gloves inside out from love's tackle,
nostrils land in nest of coiled hair—
is this the act, which shipwrecks
and destroys?

Yes, a question

Have you felt or heard breathing when no one else is nearby?
Have you felt or heard breathing when no one else is nearby?

Definitely. In fact, I almost insist on it. For nearly
twelve years I've heard Catullus breathing irregular
(verbs or otherwise)

while reading over *Carmen LXXXVII*:

Not one woman can truly say that she has been loved
as much as my darling Lesbia has been loved by me.
No faithfulness has ever been so great
in any bond of love as has been found
on my part in my love for you.

Magnificent and doomed, *Carmen LXXXVII*
became an escape attempt that failed,
remains Catullus's most haunting hour.
Years following his mysterious death in 54 BC,
his manuscript disappeared, resurfacing
in 1472 when the first printed edition of
his poems was published. Like a lexical
spectre, the poems may have haunted
Shakespeare, evident in a few of his sonnets.
Did William hear the Jacob Marley rattle of
sycophantic chains in the heights of ghastly
English haunting fashion? Ask me who I was.

And talk about lingering, does it get any
more sincerely anxious than Yukio Mishima's toy doll?
In *Confessions of a Mask*, Mishima recounts a toy in his closet
that called to him at the age of twelve. Although described as
"insubordinate," the inanimate had its own tastes and demands,
which the young Yukio began to listen to. The doll would show
Yukio images of horror, strangulations, soldiers in the throes
of mortal combat, blood pools and gory duels. Mishima ended
his career and his life in 1970 by having himself ritually beheaded
by his students, who were ordered to perform a laborious hara-kiri.

Let's not forget that by the year 1768, Bristol's Thomas
Chatterton had already conceived Thomas Rowley, an
imaginary monk of the fifteenth century, wrote and submitted work
on his behalf, which was published despite the eventual discovery
that it was fraudulent. Was Chatterton so haunted by the spirit
of an assumed fifteenth century monk that he entered his poetic heart
and gave it life? On August 24, 1770, Chatterton poisoned
himself by drinking arsenic in water.

Have you feigned or halted breathing when no one else was nearby?
Have you fainted or knelt deeply when no one else was nearby?

No. 5

loosen the bandwidth,
rejuvenate cryogenic orgasm
from actinic recovery bay
or tenant-friendly isolation chamber

With an exacto knife I count
each kiss on the grid, let us live,
L----- mine, and love "us"

as for scandal, all the gossip,
crusty and concrete,
suns can rinse infinity for us,
rust our quick witless exchange

until we break off free one denied state,
so please give me an eternity
to fill your mouth with kisses

and get dizzy from the count
for no fossil fungus
or child-labour lungs
are as loved, or would ever be

no matter the price, if haggled
or in moments I threaten to become
stone

At one point a thousand more,
our bodies angularly cocked
ready for wetwar lactic acid,
knitting kinks in hidden joints
we barely found sleep

now grown, edged out sponged
elsewhere daubed lived away,
strange how I feel connected
to a wreath rather than a ring

to be the forgotten one, or
to forget the once adored
We wear the right clothes

BETA LOVE

tweaks a brilliant tracking problem
with some Scotch Tape and brandy

consumed with talcum lips,
charmed in prickling cactus tears,

cures hunger with rich salad,
strawberries and my special vinaigrette,

drowns a sentimental rain forest
does stroke and your face glides

in regrettable forecasts; from the ghost
of the sun to the lotion the wind wears,

panic lovingly then insane
over the price of soap

    or

knot up anxious at the fear of gums
being massaged by human bristles

scalded by your callousness,
I am so afraid I run away

to the mountains and feed my body
to the famine mascot birds until I crawl

back into your cave streaked with cranberry
tears, mouth rimmed in wet sand.

I should visit
I can always run away

if you try to chainsaw my limbs off
but you know I need love.

Behind the housecoat Catullus is a medium, barrel-chested man, who, when fully dressed, likes colourful shirts open at the neck and down several buttons, for ventilating, he claims. Though his chest hair coils in a dense manner he does not exude an unpleasant hairy-chested masculinity; his cadre endorses a warm sense of comfort, intimates a general contentedness. His skin is red from constant bathing, a domestic vice he cannot kick.

Removing his yellow-red pom-pommed toque and matching mittens, Catullus brims with 100-watt excitement, compromising fingernails with an antique bite, reducing cuticles to jagged stubs, burbles on about a bunch of things in between dramatically charged celery chomps while loading a Beta tape into the VCR. Catullus makes a good case for himself, feeling obligated to list his expectations to a potential lover. Very similar to the didactic treatments found in electronics instructions. Uneasy, we are told to take a chainsaw in a torrid display of unrehearsed affection. Classify under "Hardcore Horror Art Love."

COUNTING DEAD KISSES, CRUNCH THE NUMBERS

Last night, L-----, you asked me how many kisses
would satiate my infallible tongue

As many as the straws of 7-11
stuffed into the mouths of youth

As many as coffin flies who choose to breed below the earth
where I lie, damp in the face, waiting for your plural

kiss count delivered in machine-gun terror,
or as many as the stars, when night is rural,

gazing down on the grazing sessions
of secret hummers,

lips stretched out, midriff hissed,
in unmonitored summers

As many of your kisses dished out are enough,
and more, for me, mad Catullus,

as can't be counted by jealousy
nor an evil tongue jade us

Close your eyes, admire.
Buzz kill bug kill zap nul shrill organ.

Right eye left eye weather is cold weather a system,
a thermal ballet of quick fix drama fits.

Counting kisses 1301 through 1407, the sand in the wind
a calculative cruelty helping with the additions.

Ceasing cycle deflate.
Buzz kill bug kill zap nul shrill.

Coffin flies or scuttle flies, drunk and determined
detest and survive; jerky manner hunchbacked,

jet-lagged, most active at an exposed body after butyric fermentation
and when the corpse is starting to dry. Coffin flies are most common

in buried human bodies after one year of burial. Coffin flies are able
to dig their way through cracks in the soil above buried coffins

and weather toxins, defining the cruel unmeaning of cyclical regret.
Label each grain for a faux tribute constellation that will never

appear. A coffin fly has been observed to dig to a depth of 0.5 metres
in four days, close your eyes, perspire.

Buzz kill bug kill zap nul shrill organ ceasing cycle deflate.
Buzz kill bug kill zap nul shrill.

Capable of completing their entire life cycle under the ground,
several generations can occupy a corpse without coming

to the surface. What can we get done in two months?
Two months, no months, nul shrill organ seizing dilate buzz.

It has been calculated that with 98% survival, one pair of coffin flies
in a protected place could produce 55 million flies in 60 days.

Buzz kill bug kill zap nul shrill organ ceasing cycle deflate.
Buzz kill bug kill zap nul shrill.

Even with only 1% survival, it would take only 7 months to produce
     1 million flies.
Close your dearth-fed eyes, close your dearth-fed eyes, buzz kill bug zap
     nul shrill.

No. 8
(Bang on my Heart If You Think I'm Perfect)

"O fool Catullus

stop this, stand firm, become stone"

Catullus ended *Carmen VIII* with this line to end the muse the line
has stopped me many nights in the throes of lovesickness white-
knuckled insane over a porcelain pond, flushing and clutching in a
sad bulimic throat ballet of the heart when the physical symptoms
began to dominate, I would try to trick my system by empowering
the cerebral with the words, his beautiful words, "Catullus, stop
this, stand firm, become stone," a mantra stomped around inside
me—forced denial on the body, hardening my shell allowing me to
feel from within a protected albeit imagined
layer of rock   resentir   rebuild   reregret   inappropriation
of love

No. 8
(Bang on my Heart If You Think I'm Perfect)

Born to be a sissy, digest beauty's heist, choke,
love-punched, glass-jawed, heart absorbing bleach,
everyday I feel like I'm selling it,

obdurate! shell out! for this fair Verona cyanide two-straw dance
number

PAIN PUMPS ME
HE PUMPS YOU
DOES LOVE PLUMP?

Invoice these theatrics (spoken in tear-hoarse voice)

your labia-mouth maniac is going to his dentist
tell your Catullus he has no tears, as he lowers your gitch
to say goodbye, sees the calm before the porn; your peach
sealed dry in a fresh finish
quiet, dormant as a doormat
resting up to sneak off

and dampen away from Catullus's heavy storm
& thirsty clay tongue that once motored gladly
for hours where he went just last night!
And the night before!

[Juventius wipes Catullus's mouth]

and girl, underneath ((
((spanked by Catullus no more
terse firm round and soft
terse firm round   soft
[Juventius brings Catullus tea]

Where I orbited affection, enough (I thought)
Detonate Catullus!
Whom will love you less well?
With unfit words, with lousy touch?
Who cares! This girl has flown. [Juventius rubs
the back of Catullus's neck] who will stunt double my
symphony?
As for you, gloomy cock-dead Catullus,
degenerate into something fool!

No. 9

"What's it going be then, eh?" The harsh truth of the camera
eye, like Jesus to a child, it was me and my three lunatics, that is,
Catullus, the addictive friend Rufus and the toy Juventius, and
all of us being the farthest from the warm hearth at the marble
slab table—decorated in a perky constellation of freshly plucked
cornflowers, and so we sat in The Capitoline making up our pink
sponges what to do with the night's near-whimpers that blinked as
a stern mauve chill December calculated itself insufferable

drinking the wine so close to the open flame of the fireplace,
its climate was a calming stroke

smearing expensive napkins with our cruel words, slowly
taking in the wine, holding its sinister lake portions in our mouths,
as I watched my glass get refilled, blinking past in spectral-thin
baby blue skirt with full lips red-wined and starved—for now, the
discreet younger sister of Clodia, tarting the bar with two of her
university girlfriends

yes, Mahelly—heaven-sent heaven-stole—the romantic firing
squad had been doing power squats on the front stoop of my
villa   with the rare postcard and so I had arranged this meeting
to discuss the end of the civil universe which punched itself out in
hostile jugular tugs,

our eyes, drunker than death, began to punctuate our liquored
atmosphere, a man-made terror of words and gestures and shame-
ful pantomime,

the graffiti in one of the washroom stalls I kept recalling as
Rufus gnawed away in the spotlight while Juventius caught a
glimpse of his eyes in the cutlery

the pen-chiselled words were not greeting card material, urged a
mythological promise

I have 17 testicles

Above claim, different scrawl
I'M HAPPY FOR YOU

which   wittier?

Escape artist trick voice
larynx cried for a hearse

One of the open mic poets from The Capitoline murmured to Mahelly:

> "So you're the kind of lover who only comes when it rains
>   is that what you meant by propose to your widow?"

Rufus, running his hands through his hair,
    his rouge mouth, a deflating basketball, roared into the evening;
    plotting at but failing to arrange, a solo dive without alibi

in the parking lot Catullus was no better, waiting for Mahelly to get off
her cellphone

told Juventius about his library wet dream carnal
    knowledge lodged in corduroy, "I wish it was bad daydream write off,
but no I can recall it, put Medusa's breasts into my cement mixer mouth,
while combing a lice-infested Scylla and giving head to Narcissus in a stall;
I was studying too long time, dead even longer. Great, Mahelly is off her
phoner."

    "Hey," Mahelly said, flipping her phone closed, sliding it into her
purse.
    "What did he say to you?"
    "He said, 'I was really into Asian girls for a while but I think I'm
over that now.'"
    "Oh, nice of him!"
    "What are you doing?"
    "I like your pigtails."
    "Let's go to my place."
    "Unless you prefer parks, bike paths? How about we find a
compass?"

Practical perverts Juventius and Rufus shared a bottle
of discontinued wine under Mahelly's bedroom window
heard halftone voices
Catullus made certain tequila was poured, verbs steeped in
dreary foreplay, barely there murmurs tackled by spit
never dry

No. 10

Barren laryngitis landscape, aggravated by inalterable sun.
Dry throats of this earth, vultured in fear.

Collapse. A climate of judgments are dealt with
by a nod of approval from the heavens.

Fly-spotted pupils with tears that push tiny legs
and vacant wings downstream three months now,

and the rasps of his foggy lungs stillborn play on a loop
as we sleep I watch clean night in decimal.sky.

This has become our little cluttered life,
Catullus: a suction, a destination and a mark.

You bind me to my habits so I leave you
dull at the airport, outlined in talcum powder.

But you, man residue, return, guilt washes over me.
Later on, months cloned during a calm soda raid,

I listen to your oratorical word-wrecks;
a toast-mouthed spiel on antifreeze

and aromatic bath salts, I force you into my swimsuit,
apply sunscreen with spatula. We dig meat up at the coffin

beach with suitcase keys and picnic tears. My feelings are erased
and traipsed; become a stinking far-fetched carcass.

What time are you ending? Intestina leftover love letter.
We witness weakness; vigil-tipping miscreants devalue culture

as lodged corncobs spackle sparse gums,
the next generation snorts invisible ink.

Kafka Fterkare

A restless Juventius dumps the uneaten dinner into the garbage (pasta and garlic bread, Greek salad and mussels) An abandoned tea bag cocoons in the bottom of his mug. For Juventius, the night has fallen; animal voices are concealed by motorcar sound bites, newsprint words are crimped in recycling bins, itemized refuse hallmarks the curb. Catullus has not called, has not returned, has done neither the dishes nor his other chores. Silent minutes sicken. Juventius worries, fiddles with a lock of his dyed hair above the flame. Beside two tea candles he tosses and turns in his bed, listening for the front door in anger and appropriate paranoia.

    FK FK FK FK
           embellish the journey
           dream of surgery drug permanence
           while fighting off ugly
           giant gyrating killer clams

who insist on New Age strangulation
I sigh,
as one of them plants   Kafka seeds   FK FK FK FK

           in the centre
           of my pillowcase
           and along the spine of my
           futon, I remind it, I breathe with Kafka lungs

FK FK FK FK
FK FK FK FK

                change does not
                equate improvement
              (nor do rough threats)

bedroom fashioned with poison-control mobile   FK FK FK FK FK
FK FK FK

insecticide incense, inebriated rattle
of high-end elegiac bug-spray bottles
in the height of domestic warfare drunker than the grape

FK FK FK FK

rotten food under rude fingernails,
I paw for my human remainder
and embellish the journey   as   clams swallow me whole.

The Capitoline is packed with college students and dehydrated suburban charcoal sketch drunks, the regular crowd that weasels on and off bar stools and snakes in and out of urinal poses. Catullus and his agent Harvey share a cigarette, knock back rye and ginger.

"How are things going, Catullus?"

"Things are, well, I do not like messy chores."

"Are you getting along with everyone?"

"I suppose it is that way. A sparrow was eaten."

"From what I've heard it was tofu."

"And no words from L-----?"

"How is Mahelly?"

"She's is so quickly fine, we may become acquainted in seven ways."

"So I've gathered. Any new material?"

"Just napkin sketches. This climate is doing on occasion clogged. I could say, clogged. And everyone dressing with sidewalk colours."

"Grey? Things will pick up."

"How much longer do I living there? I have been on multi times asked to the vacuum."

"Don't you like the change?"

"There is always such a thing as too much without familiar advantage."

No. 13

Rufus is medium-sized, lanky, with red hair and squinty blue eyes. While he lacks Juventius's physical humour, Rufus commands attention through a series of well thought out social pantomimes: cigarette breaks, ice cube refreshing, musical selections, or the random gamble of a text message. Though he has suffered from gout for some time from lead-lined containers and an undisciplined penchant for wine, he is able to self-medicate this ailment. When it becomes too cold in the house, Rufus puts on a layer of coats—first a noisy leather bomber (black), then a pea-green second-hand army coat with large wooden buttons he plays with while watching the news. Instead of layering up his feet in tube socks, he wears slippers. Rufus owns an immaculate jawline with which, it seems, he angles a seductive gaze. While Catullus's gaze is more intense, deliberate and seemingly without suspension, Rufus uses his as a gateway for vernacular discourse, endless, empty and sprawling topics banter out in a luminous and eloquent presentation that allows both body language and proximity to assist in social outcomes. Tonight, however, home alone, Rufus observes the dents the choreless Catullus has left in their home.

stay-at-home pest
sniffs toothpaste caps

house guest ingrown,
takes up more than half the bed

accompanied by
a scentless mould

only I can detect
and pick at,

never fully off,
always a pigmented
      remain
          der

As a silver spiralling orchard of verbal push-pins lays dormant in the living room, I watch Juventius empty his net of groceries, the phone is in the crook of my neck, "There are nights," I say, watching him with cans of chickpeas, slurping inwards my curdling cough-syrup gurgle (words oozing harlot red from my concave mouth onto the deadpan receiver), "when I inhabit the bodies of your lovers, and together," I pause, "we decide your fate, if you'll come, if you'll be touched," Juventius is now doing sit-ups, he stops, shifting his ears for better reception as

I load a didactic bear trap, "Each night, I lift the sleeping organs and peel fingerprints, label and seal them in tight jars. I talk for those you encounter in your fake pyjama love; the after-hours club of penetration you call dreaming

where primal commandments are uttered, shattered, splattered on obey, enslave your lips like a workhorse at the trough, sweat silver until makeup runs gummy." Drunk, feeling helium-odd, I clutch the telephone, the wall, my fingernails glow,

"Somehow Juventius, I know who you desire now, my brain is a reverse voodoo peephole...and I see the phallus shadow poke past my eye socket as I try to sleep; a constant windshield wiper, learning a groove inside you, ebbing my blood type from your funhouse body forever   you never had a mind, just a corkscrew and a wine-steady hand to take your pants off."

The phone drops from my grip, I clutch his stomach, fumble with precision toward his groin,   deep inside sees swollen cotton swallowed in a nightmare of dark phlegm,   drying as the final incisions of unnecessary surgery continue, in his green theatre,   this pulsing untouched body of his has no scar:

Cut the pace, session lasts just one night? Love mechanics foiled in grease, a ten-minute stretch sentenced to life in physical form, over time mental fire.

One cannot control the other
No field to play arson on
I pass out, phone cord engulfs my body;
               sweats the night through him.

Brand new grey sweatpants with a double red stripe down the leg and bright green sneakers find Juventius greeting the day after a quiet shower and tea in the kitchen. He begins to mix his hair dye and writes a short poem out on a scrap of paper on the kitchen table. Catullus, chewing on two red plastic straws, wanders by in his housecoat and notices the writing.

> Sick nervous cat on front lown
> greets the curlee day
> it is going to be good day
> to use peroxide

Catullus cackles,
"Juventius this is obsessed by yourself. I hate it. What for the breakfast? Will you cut my hair as well as cooking?"

No. 16

Juventius tries again with a piece entitled "Rome Temperature."

Cook coo
Mule moo
Pluck ox
Clove toast
Room tempurrture
Hen blender

New Tall Elegant Rich Kids

Early morning birds minus a few chime off, Mahelly in a wicked
    navy and silver
summer dress, legs taut polished by or for the male gaze (with
    double wristwatches)

has gagged
Juventius and blindfolded Catullus
on her bed   tied up extremities ceremoniously in weak
faux-leather belts,
the boys' clothing slowly chewed by bedroom floor,
plunks marbles into their navels, tells Catullus,
"I told you not to write anything for me, it's so 58 BC.

> 'If you can find an untortured space or
> quadrant in this consciousness, stretch out in
> it, plagiarize and sop it up, sooth up to, snarl
> and coo Godless; we all whimper when minor
> felons fondle us like leaky lullabies.'"

Mahelly takes the paper and squeezes it into a ball. She tightens
    the belts,
the boys are ocean-fished and ready for the sibling gobble,
or fluorescent neglect, she turns off the lights and leans into their
    ears,
speaking through the film of her lip gloss, "Catullus, I've caught
    your act, save your ink."

CATULLUS, GET A CASEWORKER

We chew with these
Where the legs bend
We hear with these
We walk on these
Used for picking things up
We smell with this
The baby sucked his ____

The upper part of the leg
We taste with this
We see with these
This covers the body
We kiss with these
Attached to the shoulder

CATULLUS, GET A CASEWORKER

Look,
once I enjoyed the
venue that
equated rich
detonation of sex

Once I wanted to be the greatest, tasteless
nurturing waster of
countless eruptions
embroiled mentor of the senseless

In my recent torpor, I have gained a trust in numbness

I clench the mischief
beneath the rug
ought to serve

L-----, I deny
You require alibis and silent
auditions of aromatic penetration

while I require
prickly situations.

II. ILL FAMILIAL

Violence is a calm that disturbs you.
Jean Genet

The Father Weeds

Wake up, neck scratched in dry aphid drool excavated from
a fine flypaper garden
viewed in near slumber, slowly the father weeds, plunks rocks
into window   drain.

      Each one he launches hits pane breaks sleep buries my
bedroom from the   outside one stone at a time, grown from
hardware store seed, his vegetation shields umbrella my sun,
I wince as my left hand crosses his grunt imprint,

roughs my temple further along throat dream soothed only in
memory sting orange Popsicle his favourite flavour minced with
dramatic degenerative qualities of impatience, impotence and
rage rolled up in memory an orange lit cigarette tip burning
a hole in night carrying me upstairs to bed, black staircase sky
tomb raids,

welcome to each searing year, recalled, time-released flashbacks,
inhale stale calendar, newsprint air as static channel clears.

Why are you telling me these things?

It was unbalanced Saturday, morning gargle overturned symphony,
another iconic fable weakening, I heard my father clearing his
charred throat in my own voice, watch me move from kennel of
talcum sheets to sandbagged eye duct smoke-stunk-spent pillows.

You were talking in your sleep last night.

I've shifted the narrative quest with little panache from paternal
to romantic in soothing anti-Oedipal post-Menendez self-induced
mind control:

Yes, in that charcoal tear theatre **d**ream where I *watche***d** it, an unname**d**
creature of *action* flew into the fountain with phantom wings

a type of moth or albino butterfly, as you calle**d** it, a **d**orm-room pixie note
tape**d** on my door   *was slowly place***d** *was slowly place***d**

Spit it out we woke up **d**espite knowle**d**ge of movement, I di**d** not put
it there, it ha**d** swarmed *was slowly place***d** it ha**d** a pollen scent a naïve
honey a trembling liqui**d**.

Fiction: several minutes this morning I have **d**one nothing
but rub the cor**d**uroy skirt at the e**d**ge of the be**d**sprea**d**
dented *in the* **d**emente**d** image of reluctant fornication.

Back to my overturne**d** paternal itch; I am born an**d** I am scol**d**e**d**. Lava hol**d**s
me. I hol**d** you close to me now, am slowly place**d** in the lukewarm broth of
uneven morning, we wade **d**eep pushing fingers

until we have a hol**d** smells like sugar or soft porn, when I start to talk about my
father you will look at my face to see numbing histrionic me, what I tell myself
what I tell myself softly what I have never met

What we **d**o, instea**d** of meeting with my father   we grow into each
other's shirts wa**d**e at municipal pools exchange   eye colours
tra**d**e on a corporeal level beyon**d** co**d**e of   genes washing instruct
ions or nutritional value menus it never en**d**s

we commute to one another; over age-ol**d**   concrete ripping
at our **d**enim commitment,

plante**d** to repel the insects who gargle suburban   crop, can
marigol**d**s plante**d** twenty years ago make a come   back?

Zucchini summers, gut-swollen in garden dangling onto   weeds
a tight out-of-print yellow cotton T-shirt suffers, the yard   cut
with scissors in dark plucked from their weak tentacles, tobacco-   fumed
tomatoes green beans too had their say in the dry tangle   family
obsessed with physical salads

non-emotions of garden all weekend he picked at virile greens
unkempt hours in sunstroke cactus in silent out-of-office experience.

Using catered hands and knees screwing the earth he toiled, sweated,
red-necked; cuticles cut soil, pinching nerves unwanted plants until one
earthy early morning tide of light witnessed him with pen sell land,

leave the weeds behind, a domestic pantomime   now with similar
movement, he has designed inside of himself,   darns his cheek

into a swollen tea bag   each year another stitch is added   in April
for his birthday I catch him   with a needle through his   cheek
dried leaves sealed in their cocoon filter,   have become temporary stubble
never drinks tea no one tells him to let it steep no one stops him no one pulls
his hand from the threaded eye and says, "Stop, David, please!"

In his big trailer backyard, overrun brutalized and plotted   against
by approved poisons, in the atmosphere of lotioned crops he is allowed
temporary space
a growth pattern.

My father's tongue is a spade, his jaw hurtles to dream   night
never pokes from earth   in nocturnal drawn bath   collapsed
into perennial shade, mimicking the path of an unrecovered   seed.

Why are you telling me these things?

Silent **d**ays **d**well between unspoken worl**d** an**d** clay han**d**s,
dental strain, intolerant facial spasms, nature working its spikes

into his properties, plant memory no further, I cannot grow this way
refuse to try, stop watering, wake.

The villa is static-crammed and sheets of fabric softener float as active hair dryers compromise the audio. The front door has been freshly touched up with a gold-fleck enamel finish. This type of bright winter morning is spent in errands and mischief. The unemployed men (Juventius and Catullus) double-glove their hands, and where scarf ends have failed to meet up, Juventius has wrapped Catullus's lower jaw in paper towel. Rufus is at a public city council meeting. Juventius wears a headband that conceals the length of his frosted bangs. He shuffles his friend down the driveway.

"Catullus, did I ever tell you," Juventius begins, "about a friend of mine who had a twin brother? They lived on the east coast, right on the ocean, and they would go fishing together for eels."

Catullus cannot imagine. "Eels? How did they meet them?"

"They swam out in the water and let the eels snake around their arms and legs. Once slithering, the boys clenched the eels and rushed out of the water, the creatures still alive as they handed them over—glistening black in the sun—to the local merchants for money, and back they'd go into the ocean, all morning, all afternoon."

Catullus balks. "That sounds like big amount work. Likely the brothers being monsters of sea time."

"They also hunted bats by clumping burdocks together into balls. They'd throw the clumps into their wings and the bats would fall out of the sky."

O Catullus sniffles, throat stitches, such contempt, so puzzled. "What the burdock?"

"It's like a spiky pine cone, those brown things I showed you, by the big pine trees. Do you recall?"

Catullus is shaking his head, his breath infiltrates his face; tongue salacious in the briny wind.

"It looks like a brown spiked bumblebee without wings or stripes. A blowfish without gills or colour."

"What they do with each bats?"

"They'd eat them."

"Now to ask you, Juventius, are we to going do a bats dinner?"

"No," Juventius says.

"Good to news, because a bats seemingly awfully full foul," Catullus says. "These make pig sounds I have heard."

"Okay," Juventius mews in agreement, simultaneously guiding the grocery cart and scanning the sales flyer. "Right, pig sounds." Drops a head of lettuce into the cart. Coins rattle, are counted, wrists are bound in plastic bags, Catullus aims himself home, dragging his feet. Juventius can hear the paper towel around Catullus's neck weaken, and with slightest reveal of a bronchial compromise O how the bath beads will be deployed: hot throat remedies, finely cut garlic slipped into tea or bath broth, kisses, play, spit on hands, holes, nipples, mouths consulted, pumping movements, an acre of lips suctioned in water   backtrack—

walk home scolded in howling auto-audio, Juventius tells Catullus more about the brothers, how one would spit on his peas, the other, his lamb chops. "Why?"

"One liked the vegetables, and one liked only the meat, so at dinner, before they'd start they'd spit on the things they didn't want the other brother to eat, in case they had to go to the washroom, or weren't paying attention at the table."

The villa is pregnant with sun and dust. While Catullus unpacks the groceries, Juventius takes a moment while running a bath and looks out the open bathroom window; bleached blue backdrop allows him to see infinite the bat wings, burdocks, sticking to wing ebbing, organism hurtling to forest floor, hapless quarry.

This youthful bounty acts on a loop; the brothers in nature, free, recycling murder—seeing what he has never seen, only what he was told, Juventius's mental makeup quicksands elsewhere, he is bloated into another sensation—the muscles in the back of his legs clench tight as he releases a new wave, into the bath he skins his memory.

Juventius plans his evening with push-ups, pea-soup-can arm curls, numbs Catullus with valerian root tea. Reads the folded sports section:

> Soccer is a natural game and although the Romans may not have played team soccer there are references to boys kicking balls around in the streets. Cicero described one court case in which a man getting a shave was killed when a ball was kicked into the barber. The ball must have been an inflated pila.

Later, still cozy, Juventius's bare legs descend the stairwell to the laundry room in the basement. He does all his clothing, every last stitch. The floor is peppered in detergent, not snow, as Catullus calls it. "Juventius, weather is now everywhere," Catullus says, laughing, with his hands fisted deep into the guts of the box of flakes.

"Why can't you water the plants in the kitchen and hallway?" Juventius asks, separating black socks from white dress shirts and face cloths.

Catullus stands with a half-yawn, reading the side panel of the ripped box; gripping it tightly. "Please tell how this clean clothes, Juventius?"

And Brother, for all Time, Hail and Farwell[3]

My brother, unhappily removed from me,
our whole house buried along with
Glenvale Boulevard, broken
into four grocery hearse boxes,
crusts cut off, dried up

Lapide candidiore diem notare
(to mark with a white stone the luckiest days)

once we in our driveway drew
(to detract real estate)

with expressive white chalk
body outlines infantile
suggesting murder,
revealing our hostility

And since it is so,
I wouldn't want you to decide
that I'm doing this out of spite
or lack of appropriate
generosity,

I would produce it unmasked,
I cannot keep silent the auction
enhanced with attitude, aged
in a cellar of false-bottomed bourgeois
apathy—

3 *Frater, ave atque vale!* is the last line of *Carmen CI*. In 57 BC, Catullus left for a year to go overseas to join the staff of Gaius Memmius, new governor of Bithynia. It was a much needed rest for two reasons: first, the news of his brother's death had reached him from Verona, and, second, L----- had betrayed him.

I've been burning, like the overpriced
poached waters of
Malis in the hot gates of Mount Oeta,

my eyes contain faint love shrapnel
have not stopped wasting away in
driveway tears, my cheeks have not
stopped being wet

I'm dominated by the nautical sensation
of our severely unfit weather cracking
our parched bike path fields,
bonding the igloo breath
of toboggan swamp runs
or stick sport marathons

all congeal in thumbprint Kodak
stain sweet comfort, like watching
a black tornado from a safety channel,

when the house innards had fallen,
with an unerring arrow, stirring and
bursting the yoke of marriage—

emptied into
our unwashed pockets,

we walked through one another,
ignoring the cranial x-rays,
DNA code that once read
minds, detected pain,
        absorbed need.

Autoburglary

a) I grew up in a city in a neighbourhood full of flimsy meatloaf fat. That greyish cat food goo that just bobbled off the old meatloaf brick. The summer months bubbled and stained newsprint brown. In their respective boxes, the newsprint would cook and burn the hands of its readers. Sometimes everything smelled like that, or the complete opposite, which at my age was bright grape pop. I grew up in a city in a neighbourhood full of chipped teeth, skinned knees and this is where I learned to proofread spit in my mouth or to lubricate scrapes, the dirt, blood and torn tissues with the spit of others.

b) In the sun at recess, the boys in public school sharpened their dicks on pop can tabs, bent with crooked teeth and split lips. They compared dick size, or pissed together on Saturdays on the red brick school walls. Or from the rooftops until the custodian came. They were up there getting tennis balls from the previous week's recesses. They all huddled for perverse measure. For years and years. Wind through their hair, freckles darned in sun. Through fads of BMX bikes, skateboards, mountain bikes; hair worn to reflect TV pin-ups, highlights. Then the clothing: tapered pants, stone-washed jeans, shirts with tiny horse over one nipple, elastic-waist boxers covered their dicks, which they sharpened all through childhood in order to one day stab girls for sex. Stabbing was the sound their tiny Dungeons & Dragons cast-iron knights made against basement stomachs. That cold place. Or the sound the sheers beat down despite rusty overgrown hedges. In the alleys, the bits of green hit the concrete from neighbouring backyards. The boys knew what stabbing looked like because of the dirty books they found in the garbage bags full of hair behind the barbershop. The alley held them tight. In the bag, the magazines tanned, as if to further perfect the centrefold. To dissolve any tan lines.

Tanning in the afternoon taught us all how to make ourselves come and shake. This is what we liked. We grew to like it, it was the cure for countless go-nowhere knee scrapes, puppeteering toy-car chases.

c) It's just a note, perhaps to illustrate that although chemically processed foods nourished us in synthetic orgies of Saran Wrap and carbonated lemonade, we admired the vegetarianism of our hamsters and gerbils. We relished the silent-auction façade of our goldfish living in ultimate time-bomb surrender. Never exchanging harsh words, the goldfish and we existed as ants and earth, sun and skin, fist and pane of glass. No. The last relationship had to do with my temper, my relentless-at-six anger. I cut my hand on this friend's door and he said to me how I would forever have less blood than he, and how I'd never catch up to him, and I washed in the bathroom, the blood down the drain and my paling face in the mirror. I've bled since; however, I have no accurate number, and no longer have contact with Brian, whose glass door cut me open and stunted my spiritual growth.

No. 24

Valerian root was plucked from the Priapus section, as I sniffed its dirty-sock scent, Catullus began to shake in fatigue, his eyes half-cocked,   his yawns exaggerated gargled in names and laughter.

In the back of the health food store, the proprietor's daughters smoked clove cigarettes; where black stiletto shoes were returned by a friend from the previous night, where I spoke no words, where the daughters, elegant in decor, had tight backs to me, stretched then shifted weight, we followed the terse curves for direction,

they spoke in German to one another, scratched at their bras until Catullus had passed out completely, I wiped wet from his lips, revived him next to a wall of scented soaps.

Everyone was on the pimpled streets in lines of mascara and cologne, warmed up for their pedestrian shift as gears or oiled cogs, in a grind of movement. A woman led us into a pay phone and squeezed at our balls, we still had our pants on.

"We have friends to meet," one of us said, "we can't stay long,"

> we welted each other, mouths clumped in vending machine
> cake & eggs
> orange tongue carved breath as we kissed, I drew us a
> battle plan out of us, spit on the coiled wires of us
> Catullus looked up at the pay phone's throat, moaned indifferent.

"Did you know that person?"

"In the phone booth? Either way, the Gods do not visit earth anymore. On this quarry, excessive and exposed sphere, vulnerable scapula is part of the dining pallet; fathers grind daughters, murder sons to seduce daughters-in-law, husbands throw wives ten storeys from balconies, media illuminates the vigils, cheats the shot, rich hump poor without muskets, bodies are buried in the neighbour's lavish goldfish ponds, and I hold up the coke-dusted mirror."

Outside of a nightclub, well-groomed bodies got along, waded by the bouncers, a towering denim gargoyle posing, sneezing on Catullus and Rufus hours of taco steam fast food rodents, expired subway transfers billowing in the vacant arid moments of our lives.

Without language, the small man offered Rufus and Catullus a bouquet. I remember nudging Juventius, who was munching a mango on a stick. "Check out Rufus," snarling at the flower vendor, feeling pregnant, but man, Catullus laughed so hard, tears swaddled his eyes.

Later that night, I hide my pee-stained toga in my closet, brush my teeth and spit the red wine down the drain, stand by my bedroom window and hold an empty ice cream container of water over my garden.

I'm eight years old, watering Styrofoam cups in which mung bean seeds have been carefully thumb-planted. My name is Juventius and has been Juventius all along. As this is now my mess, my responsibility, I watch Juventius (me) shudder in shame; his parents are yelling and it's a school night. I keep pouring the water over the Styrofoam cups, drowning the crops. Tears race out of his face, my face. His father pounds on the kitchen cupboards, and Juventius feels it in his stomach and cannot swallow anymore. The Styrofoam cups overflow and bits of dirt pour over the sides. He pees his pants, wipes his tears but smells blood. He closes his eyes tightly around his heartbeat. He staggers down the stairs; his parents' screaming is crossed by the television's unrelenting static. Into the kitchen he tiptoes, dripping blood and concern; Juventius picks up his throat from the meat slicer, bits of it still cling to the blade, while others have been spat out across the dirty floor.

I am wearing a red sweater with a yellow duck; my cheeks are red, my eyes tiny and squinty and my nose a button. I am wearing clean socks and a tight shirt with a collar under my sweater, but the colour is now flecked in caked blood. I am not at the restaurant with my family. I know I'm supposed to be; I know that it is why I'm dressed up, but I am alone and I have lost a lot of blood. If I am dreaming. I walk from a storage area enclosed in the scent of powdered mustards and I look up to the tranquillity of the wooden beams until I am out into the main dining area, looking for a familiar face. The blood is gone, the tears are dry and have left my skin red and pawed.

MOM DRAWS AN INFLUEUNZA BATH

whimperment
microbes hyphenate
deliberate inebriate

after-school special
meeting wool mittens
yarntongued:

activism pamphlets in plentitude
shy away home-schooled

throats open marriage
miraging bronchial chamber

clogged then communal:

plague us
maul us
grievous is panacea?

dismantle a scaffold's intent;

for Juventius it is always autumn
cannonball cannabis
sold September scholarly

a) It was probably a major holiday. b) White wine gave his mother a headache. c) The father was drinking again. d) The father was drinking for a thousand years. Then another. He would not say if it was deliberate. e) The lamp was weak, and dusty was the lampshade. The father sat next to it except when the dinner guests ate. f) His youngest son, Catullus, never lost count: cribbage, bridge, chess, broken dinner plates, nose picks. g) Julius Caesar was over one night, then another (left a lot of peas on his plate; "They looked like guillotined army men," Catullus once remarked). h) Liver spots fashioned themselves unalterable; ornamental gravy stains designed the men in their separate stupor. i) No one was the wiser, no one cried but baby Catullus—sometimes his brother. Can Juventius sleep over? j) No, Catullus, you haven't even met him yet. k) With the leftover dough the brothers baked apple pies. l) With the leftover tinfoil the brothers constructed crowns. m) Some autumn nights the brothers would roast pumpkin seeds with their mother, after gutting the orange planet. n) The father didn't suffer them, had game rage, even when no game was being played. Somewhere he knew a game was on. o) Guests sometimes stayed for coffee and bridge. p) He threw his hand down, dramatic, flushed, strewn with failure, everyone saw the cards land in the dip: J K 6 8 Q A 10. q) What do you mean what kind of dip? r) Caustic lip act. s) Gulp act. t) Gulp war. u) "I'm going to jar your tears." v) "I'm going to jar you in tears." w) "I'm going to jar you to tears." x) You can tell by the smell of the cold gravy. y) You can judge from the malicious photographs. z) It was probably a major holiday.

FAMILY PLOT NO. 2

One morning insane red discount plaid shirt madman dug up backyard with phantom passion: like a lover hollers into deep holes, as if he buried himself then had second thoughts and helpings of tantrum

Spark plugs removed from the family car, the illicit surgeon, paternal gardener of unfit weeds with rage nutrients under cuticles, pocketed for later, I motivated the wooden tray planked it across his back, ran heckling quick to neighbours. Mom in the police car doing post-match commentary looking up, cigarette turret in his mouth, replacing the spark plugs, officer lowering head, suggesting he "cool off"

"They're letting him go?"

"He's going to his parents' house," the officer said. Later in the afternoon I did push-ups, phoned my best friend over, who brought a bat, we drank soda on the front steps, mom made us banana bread. Once love may have flown their kite knot today knot ever ending mom sad day Photostat itself, reshuffled periodically no wind at all and suddenly a gust, a tumbleweed. Imagine that you spun a huge woollen man and sat him down at the dinner table, his arms, legs and neck all gobbed in gravy, his woolly texture clashing against all we strived to be.

FAMILY PLOT No. 3

Once you told me the neighbourhood kids stole your skipping rope, it was 1953, the end: knotted wooden handle would never stare into your black-olive eyes again. Forty years forward, nothing is as stolen as time, upgraded photographs chart decline, together we are visiting your mother at the decrepit elderly lodge.

Depression was a magnet, regret a valve, with giant camcorder I frantically document mood; each sizzling overheated frame on the fourth floor zoom crisis, panning the dresser, light fixture, handmade birthday cards, anything but her frailty, pabulum mind or medicated banter.

Picking up her tiny audio, "too many bananas," you tell her, makes her fat, "every other day," you suggest coldly, encourage exercise, movement, she surrenders to sheets and baby powder, tells the room, "When you were little, Diane, you got alligator and elevator mixed up…. *Are we taking the alligator?* you would ask me."

"I'll see you next week," you say, spent, derailed, prepare final hour, insure comfort, adequate concern, "it's important to remember the good times," you tell me. I wait in the alligator's stomach in silence while you speak with a nurse. We take the alligator all the way down.

III. ANTIQUE MOOD DISORDER

I believe that I am in hell, therefore I am there.
Arthur Rimbaud

Urban Tumour Patterns

Deadpan Quick List Draft 1

Ammonia ulcer ointment by appointment only,
tarpaulins manicure set, wind-resistant rent control
pegs, 40-watt blood clot cheesecloth heart thermometer
lightening bulbs.

Truth about families;
no one marries deadpan,
food silences consuming goods
satiates tension temporarily

in Domestic Olympic chores,
success is based on the bartering
child or spouse.

Should we bring the dog? is an event,
I'm starving, I need cigarettes,
buy more trophy wife polish.

Soaked pets rain caves in
expensive manes.

Deadpan Quick List Draft 2

Mussels tighten unselling, late in the close shift
quilt drying cement, fluoride water buffalo'd
milk of amnesia low-fat thumbtack, spiritual
dyslexia pabulum.

Overscore underscore oven mitts
and hide your "original crease"
high-school misogynist H-bomb love letter:
Dear Graffiti tits,

Open 24 Hours.
However long this urban tumour kneads
to steep in its state of alarming sustenance.

ATTIS SHRUGGED

Tied outside the electronic eye door once and for all
dog-torn Attis pissed on plastic rabid animal statues,
his testicles coughed up in tornado-soft sneezing fit
while we small talked 8 ITEMS OR LESS.

"What does Cybele have to say now?"
"About all this plastic surgery?"

Gauze sloths bright in grocery store within linoleum
webbing eyes digest small fingertips squirming
for a can of corn mass tenants, future tantrums,
obsessed with obese with chickpeas no one screams
you are all repetitive mutations aisle four all continuous
I am a Darwin sketch with a coupon for yogurt.

Attis, loom your cries in Phrygian woods, love-tossed
sicko, down thumbtack malts, wail, curl your toes
in pond mud mask, smell hurt skin, flake into ventriloquist
sponge,

ears perk,
runt you are chants,
axe you swing swoosh.

Squabbling familial units in poached cotton scowl glossy
in attire flimsy even, uneven dementia, soggy coupons
polluted minutia of convenience;

we are part of something
we are part   something
here at the Pollux & Castor Hypermart.

Outside raw and plump,

Attis barks midriff
rips and sniffs,

examines his fingernails,   nibbles the remains   of toast
particles as sparrows circle   curious, waiting   to share in
the dine, dive in on the dry oral potion to be coaxed   down
tiny bird throat, Attis, snow   is attaching itself wet to your
system, inside nervous, depressed,   I count the scratch marks
on Catullus's back examining the depths of each mission as my
grilled cheese grills inside plastic bag, I won't see you for five months,
Attis, coaxed down teary man throat, our miserable eyes in sympathy
slings, clash furious in the   stairwell, I have cashed in on your scent;
you break free from the leash,   walk to your car, I into the wall,
verbs absolved regret is non-language,   a faceless stampede of
accruing nausea, my living my lively wood, my living will prequel.

I listen by   inflatable woods,   kneel beside parked cars,
and subscribe to deranged pamphlets like *Shivering Oblivion*
and germinate   in low-sodium anxiety supplements.

Fumble with ingredients.
Get the soup right.
Convince you upright.

Drive mad one way drive mad one way not mine.
Drive mad   way drive mad   way not mine.

Keep on deleting, Attis,   press lukewarm digits,
I have shoplifted life,
pulse, in order to make good, chaotic sweat between us,
how you ask?
by taking off   your layers with   such accurate stunt words.

No. 31

Alone Juventius enters the art gallery, its white walls at first soothe, then, as his focus sharpens, the bright tone shapes his curiosity. The installation is loquacious. Along the four walls eight porcelain jaws rest on horizontally fitted white wooden circles. Four other patrons move between the jaws, lowering their heads and turning their necks to the front teeth. Each set of teeth is decaled in smashed-up bits of cellphones, resembling homemade braces. #32 546 01 9 7*
8 6 525 #1299

Gum lines are bordered in digits, front teeth eclipsed with keys like 8 or pound (#). Juventius passes each jaw, noting the small placard in front of the display with the text message written out in a clean bold font. As he passes a jaw, he triggers a gargled voice, mechanically spewing a random text message verbally.

IS THAT AN INVITATION?
CALL ME I'M ALONE NOW.
WORKING?

He circles the gallery once more, careful not to set off the voices.

Juventius walks home in one large gust, as leaves,
plastic refuse and rock orbit his coat, then ricochet off his trouser legs.

No. 31

Eager to be held, the room is harsh, swollen with the mood
    of aching jaws.
The room is conditional; its look is the same as
your body—replicated in plaster and broadloom,
actions recoil and brim on the sex surface, paint is wet,
dries up.

The room is told by its dentist of receding gums,
    of broken crowns, of bad grinding habits.
Two pimples, a sweaty pair of boobs, a desire to weigh
them in this magnificent heat, heaving in judgment.

An undercurrent of hurtled poses are retired
after sixteen clever acts.

DESPONDENCE COURSE

Ferocious wind pushes fertilizer
into my mouth,
my new spade hits earth.

From my bulb nursery heist,
I slide *Babiana Stricta* hybrid
into its womb, with promises of leggy
maroon sprawl.

Flush to nostril, engaging sensory system
of adult male who occupies host's body.

Bound for guaranteed turmoil
and clamp-mouthed, it lubricates,
platoons its stance
on the trip-wire hemline:

    sit closer
    be closer
    like want call
    walk by my house
    lioness,
    blow me
    up eat my remains
    delicious figment
    of relaxation cascade
    over frostbitten
    ungloved paws.

Meticulous behind in black cotton holster
painted star flush to cheekbone
engaging sensory system of adult male
who occupies the host's body.

       Is

bound for conditional recoil
and clamp-mouth, it necessitates,
maroons lament
on the hot-wired fence line.

No. 33

Catullus enters the villa after a day of snow shovelling, eating from his ground-beef sports sock and watching the Santa Claus parade at Mahelly's house. She wears a cotton one-piece leotard; during the commercial breaks he would pat her firm plump bottom, holding back scarring bites with tiny kisses. At the home front however, a variation on the treachery found in Carmen LXXVII *infects the vignette; Catullus finds himself orbiting resentment toward his friend Rufus. It just feels right.*

Face combed of snow, Catullus enters the home slightly in song. The wet flirty words of Mahelly still fresh and hard linger—for it was so sensual and rigged with delight! As he rubbed her from behind, he lowered his face into her crotch, inhaling deeply. "What does it smell like?" she asked, reminding him how wet she was. "Muffins, cookies, cake," he replied into the back of her neck.

Face combed of scarf, staggers into the hallway: "Rufus, my friend, for nothing and in vain I trusted you," and continues, one sock deflating at the foot: "No, not for nothing, but rather at a high and painful price that chafes. How convenient and without lubrication do you slither in and burn my guts."

"What now? Why are you all wet?" Rufus asks.

"I fell."

"Where? Where did you fall?"

Catullus whips his scarf into Rufus's face, stomps his feet, sniffing the warm cooking air. "Call me the make-out king!" Catullus proclaims, his hand triumphantly clenched as if holding a sabre.

Rufus shuts the refrigerator door and returns to the hallway. "I'm not calling you anything... Whack-off king, maybe."

Catullus fishes around for something in his pocket.

"Rufus, I went out today and bought the things for heat box."

"That box is called a microwave."

"I purchased thing to cook at our favourite store now that after I played with Mahelly."

"Oh?" Rufus pauses. "How's that going?"

"At her couch after shovels snow-snow watched Santa street parade. Do you know this route? He is red and old into children's house to eat. On the screen, thousands children drooling windy."

"You missed dinner. What else have you been doing? I haven't seen you in days."

Catullus pulls his crusty sports sock from his pocket, slapping it down on the kitchen counter. "I ran out meat."

"That's the most gross," Rufus says, trying not to look the deranged garment in the eye.

"And, unlucky me, steal all our pleasures, all meat gone, you foul friend."

"What pleasure? There are some leftovers, heat them up in your friend, the *heat box*, if you'd like."

"I will need more tomorrow, maybe I find new sock for that."

"No, don't do that anymore; people will think you are not well."

"You have stolen, O heartless poison of life, O plague on friendship, call me the make-out king and scorn my fortune in betrayal."

Rufus still says no. "No, you stink, I don't get it, you take so many baths and you still stink. And your hair, what's happening there, Catullus? Let me cut it for you."

"I fell in garbage, garbage day here today, it was popular."

"You are not supposed to fall in garbage."

"I kissed Mahelly and she kissed me. Everywhere, I kissed her ass, punctuated tongue. Her hole looks like a tiny balloon knot."

Rufus scrubs the pot, eyes the dish towel, his hands drip. He dries them, licks his lips.

"She smells like olive oil and candy."

"I have to make a call."

"She choked my finger with her ass. Where is Juventius?"

"Out at the movies I think, or an art show. Can't remember. Hold on," Rufus says, dialing the phone as he tucks himself around the hallway. His voice wanes and dries out, "Okay, I'll see you at two then, get some rest," Rufus says.

While loading his sock, Catullus stares into the refrigerator's light, vacant but focused at the task. "You have stolen, O heartless poison of life, O plague of friendship, dead as driftwood."

want to hear about the colour the salad dressing wore
when it hit his lips
    or
witness a cat-eyed lust-spasmed facial pose thrown back
seventeen minutes later?

slow-motion technology takes poetic
recollection to new heights of

    a) consciousness
    b) consequence
    c) accuracy
    d) narcissism
    e) cruelty
    f) subjectivity
    g) liticaphobia

The paper bag contains one Greek salad, with extra olives. "I like playing with them in my mouth," Mahelly offers, a line almost vetoed in a meeting, four months earlier.

A full bathtub topped off with a small amount of foam, no pause or knock, he feels her inside, breathes on the doorknob before entering. In her mouth a hair elastic dangles until called for,

nightmarish sliding of the bathroom door, the aromatic bath salts, eyelashes treading in a still bath of mascara, she blinks, vanity forms a sweaty queue,

she kisses him, taking a spoonful of honey in her mouth, she feeds him the mixture. "Are we sharing that salad or what?"

Mouth drips onto free hand, undoes belt buckle, stands up, pants fall down completely unbuttoned wriggles out of denim skin Mahelly up from belly, snake pose, naked stomach hits tiles,   lemon juice squirts from lips, she drips over her chin, into his mouth, her tight wet-fresh body cries, "I'm your salad."

No. 35

At the bar, Mahelly just blurts out, "He's so dumb," twitches her nose at Catullus, who stands awkwardly admiring the shape of her skull. She is still laughing, pointing to her male friend, and all Catullus can think about is time, heartbeats, how those two properties weave in and out of each other—Mahelly's tongue blinks through her bright wall of teeth. "Not bright at all," but that doesn't stop her, she likes them dumb. "You pick them. Like dominating." It's her narrative slant, lip gloss or not, with two fingers the straw is steered into her mouth, skin well adorned in fragrance and invisible jealous fingerprint stains, lucky love culprits. She wades slowly to the music, but does not dance. Her blouse mouth exudes a cinematic coherence, an unerring focal point, waiting for words, shoplifted kisses, flints from her shtick, the Eros-driven vanity in her grade-eight pigtails, the soggy crotch tales of her teenaged lifeguard years. "Do you like soggy crotch? I don't miss it," and those cavity-blue eyes boring through Catullus not nervous not calm.

The next day, in the late afternoon, Catullus rejects the first size of the cut. The butcher slices the salmon on top of the pellets of ice. The dense pink in his hand, so absolute, as if after he swallows the meat this particular colour will not exist ever again.

PHALLIC LUNATIC

His mouth is marked with raccoon paw scratches
when I put a soft damp cloth on his lips, I hear
the night outside growl nocturnal delight.

While we castrate the moon
undoes our pants and coaxes
us into slumber,

the clock's miniature heartbeat soothes us,
calms the evil we first mapped out in the car's interior.

Renew the lawn, smear the driveway with canteen water
cleanse those hosed-down clawed urban pedestrians who
cackle, listen carefully to the clockbeat; it holds them together,
pulses on their wrists and teeth: brush lifeless sunless skin
feathered with veins. The impossible yellow string stained with
grease hardens; it's December   heads tilt to the black
blindfold of sky, centring bright   point sliced white ammunition
lodged in a dark barrel sky.   I detect nicotine on his breath.

He is still when he smokes   hairs on his arm sway in a melee
coral reef of static. His pro   fessional body adjusts to the collar
of his blue dress shirt. His   hands pollute my lips. Then divide.
A thief would have him   enslaved to tread cement with words
and trade. A pusher would   have him fenced in with fear and necessity.

His heel grazes the accelerator—soon we enter the chamber, feel his close shave,
ten-thirty. School night. Pale steel illuminates nostalgia. Headlights shake, swell.
Ready with open mouth to clean the barrel. Hand limp, tightens over purple, pink
and wait beyond the steel moon to be fired.

INVESTMENT FOREPLAY

1.

this is a suicide note not a petition
get your own pen and parchment

it began with flower delivery:
the time of the month when tiger

lilies arrived, Mahelly bled on them
like delicate fingers

I want to run with you on the mountain and be your killer,
but not a killer of love

(do you know I comprise critical notes on earth's
infrastructure, the way produce lies in barrels, I do
police sketches, I match lip-tips, the scent of skin)

do not box office coffin me
on a postcard with a kissy thumbtack

I will lie to you forever
awake me with investment

foreplay your tomorrow morning breath
chew the elastic as you finger the menu

2.

will wilts me
spills and splits me

teeter taught me
knead my knot

spree in mouth
tea zips, shouts

fill a float pill drives
a tongue drill

leave a neck puckered
tie a moan to a cloud

drip from love
ride me

spent lover over-
cast

3.

our clothing in ditches
lips full of glitches

blood is this year's vintage:
a salty excrement wine

almond finger nails
plant then seed

into sulk skull
a collective incision

caramels its altruistic
post-intercourse depression

valve rare, well done
love tugged, we race

to our suicide survey course,
call it a day.

Temporary Lust Supplement

Treasure the wound; cherish its cohesive state, its topical status.
Envy red puffy synergy, its vulnerable theatre, as odorous

cure-alls clog nose of room, it was like the poem to a napkin thief
Catullus wrote, a rotten dinner guest who made off with—

Perhaps someone sat on it, disappeared in a pocket or curve.
Cherish its cohesive state, topical status,

ache over the missing napkin, in our daily lives.
Each moment we breathe, "pass me a napkin,"

our inner Catullus does inventory, forever domestic,
nostalgic, hung up on all the wrong things.

Envy the red puffy synergy, sopped-up sleeve of red wine.

CARMEN LIGHT: XC, CI, LXXXIX, IIA, LXXVII, LXXXI, XCIII, XCIX, LXXXV, LXXVI

XC: FAMILY TIES

Mothers knit sons
spike dangerous nature.

CI: BROTHERSHIP

But brother; my ship without
you, so young its belly not
monstered, how we no more
laugh or teeter on hilltops,
toss burdocks to bat wings,
or torture frog bellys with
our rocks all suffering. In jail
comic strip search I'm finished
without you spoon & dissolved
burning shooting nose of
winter, brother move closer
to my arrowhead heart.

LXXXIX: LICORICE WHIPPING BOY

Gellius is licorice-thin, no shit.
His family works him over more times
than a teenage hand doing homework!

Never see them at the dinner table,
always brushing their teeth, sniffing
leftovers, picking hairs from each other's gums.

IIA: HARDCORE

How low does your
girdle growl? Landing on
the core of a golden apple,
swiftly digested.

LXXVII: THE LOW ROAD

Rufus, less clever stunt cock,
admire the pawned flesh,
tweak your willing lust slave,
dine on monotone dust mites,
unskilled sex actors overrehearse
bobbing and gargling in the awful hours
who drown real love, then kiss the brine;
both of you will suffer in these poems for all time.

LXXXI: I THOUGHT YOU WERE MY BOYFRIEND?

Juventius, with whom did you go to the movies? I can
see the kernel artifacts in your teeth—smell more on
your breath. Whose voice is that, raspy and blinking on the
answering machine?

In the bathtub my court will decide your fate, a torture
planned: toaster or touching.

XCIII: CONSERVATIVE PARTY

Stephen Harper, I am not particularly
obsessed to side with you,
or know the colour of your silk tie.

XCIX: EYES OF A DART

Playing darts with your tongue,
Juventius, encourages me to make
marks on a scoreboard
I keep hidden.

LXXXV: ABSOLUTES

C+L+H= I feel tormented

deal in absolutes
meander between
hydraulic—angelic

gummy were those heart strings
because, *he thought*, "a friend is a
haemorrhage you'd like to forget"

hustle me this sparrow boy:

did you *love* and *hate*
to cancel out those properties
or bounce a romantic cheque
                    deliberate?

LXXVI: MEMORY GLANDS

memory glands
let out the hem—
locusts pocus
defiance fiancé,
I want to shed
the teeth of this
ache,
each cavity,
each kiss;
a chaste paralysis.

IV. BROKEN ROMAN SCENE

Whom the gods would destroy they first make mad.
Euripides

Radio

From what I heard she got a baby by Quintus M. Celer
My best friend says she used to fuck with Rufus,
I don't care what none of y'all say I still love 'er.

Chorus

get down girl go head get down (I'm already dead)
get down boy go head get down (I'm already dead)
get down girl go head get down (I'm ready dead)
get down boy go head get down (Can't feel a thing)

[COMMERCIAL BREAK]

a contrast in styles
two losers congeal
motel sheets in June
consummating a shallow
fit on hormonal bloodletting

words quick leech, tenderize
it is all body
it is called body
render lungs vociferous,

word-sick, word-sink
commands fail, fulfil,
security is a vapour
trust is a powder
snort the barely
visible scratch
baring all

ORNATRIX ON FIRE

Clodia's room is distended as peach and lime tones filter through the
thick silk curtains. Outside, the faint sound of schoolyard banter washes
up against her bedroom window. The sun squeezes new colour into the
heavily perfumed room. Though it's six hours before the art opening,
Clodia is rushed. At the mirror, she speaks to her hired hands and sings
sickly, "La-di-dah, Ornatrix on Fire, la-di-dah, set your tits on, oh my,
pretty, do your job well or kiss some flames tonight...la-di-dah,

"*Ornatrix on Fire*, it's the working title, what do you think?
Never mind. Just hurry up, and don't screw this up for me.
Fear, tremble, but do your job, sweetie pie,
or I will tear your heart out
with a crooked plumber's wrench,
punch your breasts for the heinous crime,
please hurry up, do not screw this up."

With refined choice of chalk, white lead, pale vermilion,
rouge, the extract of crocodile, eye-shadow, boxing of ash,
powdered antimony saffron or black lead, toxic condiments no
modern lady would use.

Breast bands applied, strophium or mamillare,
the long white stola drawn in at the waist, sea green,
azure blue, Tyrian purple, shoes supple white leather or—

"I want the purple ones.[4] Pardon? Well, if you saw them
in Mahelly's room go fetch them now!

---

4 Open-toed pumps. It was not uncommon for women of power
to discipline their house servants, ornatrix or slaves. Some
hot-tempered ladies would beat (with hairbrush) or burn the
nervous girls if a ringlet of hair was out of place. This was not
uncommon, especially if pain was inflicted accidentally during
a routine manicure.

I'm responsible for so much," Clodia flings Shakespeare
into the air, the words scream as the book lands spine up.

SONNET CXVI

If this be error and upon me proved,
I never writ, nor no man ever loved.

"Tell me, pretty; yes, you, bubble-bum, how one line
could have made it down without all this fuss
right here? Make me hot hot heat! A thousand necks
will kink tonight, attached to my strut, aching to be
touched." [5]

5 Even the politicians were drawn to Clodia's extreme beauty.
Cicero publicly compared her to Hera the Goddess. Clodia was
also an exquisite dancer.

EFFLUVIUM SHOT

"Now," Catullus says, snorkelling through his speech,
"my sperm is tornado-dormant, with the assistance of
   buckwheat[6] pyjamas, L-----, I am weak, I met your sister
   Mahelly.[7] When will the wilted hour whip me?"

The moon would hang as awkward;
an unfit testicle lumped in a leather sheet,
deliberate, exotic, but still cruel.

Accompanied by harmonic tremors
of his famous accounting jingle,
revisited, remastered, remixed
for the new age of global intercourse

gangly naked nostalgic, he texts,

"Give me a thousand kisses and
 a thousand more, my calculator
 is solar, my appetite for digits giddy."

6 Buckwheat is a libido-curbing herb.

7 Mahelly remains a literary construct, holding up the beams of
the immorality play into which Catullus has been injected. Clodia
was rumoured to be at the audition where "Mahelly" was cast as an
honorary sister. In truth all three of the sisters were named Clodia,
and all were married. The husbands: Metellus Celer, Marcius Rex,
and Licinius Lucullus, a millionaire and bibliophile.

New Lesbia Cylce

THAT'S IT! *Lesbia faxes Catullus five of her "dug up" poems. Juventius reads the poems first, carefully handing each page to Catullus who sits nauseous on the couch. Catullus sips on his valerian root tea. After handing Catullus the last of the faxed pages, Juventius returns to culinary excellence: chops clean vegetables, boils potatoes, marinates lamb and opens a tin of lentils for a magnificent stew.*

CLEANING THE BATHTUB WITH BLEACH

memory drives its wagging
tongue; a bath of hornets
crushing wings,
bursting mechanical eyes

CATULLUS, NO CATHARSIS

punishment alludes me
no new knowledge can be
extracted from false
DNA testimony

---

lexically/sexually
leading him on
letting him go
has meant nothing

FLOSSING

pestilence inside the silence
pestilence or *pestisilence*

squeeze a face for juice
all is plague
all is plaque

not hard enough
too emotional,
like my sponge

EATING DISORDER IN THE SECOND PERSON

scoundrel casserole add dinner guests
fussy lover, I could not invite you
to my barbecues, not because my chairs
have splinters

      ---

tormented were the termites,
bulimic with sawdust projectile
please don't yawn, you jealous
toothpick

STARING CONTEST

we cut holes
in January snowflakes
blinked enough to know
this was no ending

MEAT IS MURDER

My body is now a typ o
yours published, best-selling
translated and sold into other
languages
praised, boxed,
reissued,
evacuates my carpal touch.

More copies leave each day
identidem identidem
I remain liticaphobi c,
and do not answer the living.

The destructiveness of self-probing, you want to cry out just to keep going. The amusement park is vacant and no one can hear you because everything is a prearranged representation: cartilage, motion, pose, persona, glandular discharge under the arms and on the tummy, attitude, temperature, altitude in the moment, perhaps one you've lived or forgotten, until now.

This is **N-V**, the new author ride at a broken amusement park, purring and praying you'll get on it, fall tranquil, upside down, from the seat.

JERK COUGH

Mahelly is back from a teacher's conference where, during wine-fogged temper tantrums, she milked the moaning upright members of campus libraries, who tricked her into detention, now the moist May morning gurgles, fresh orgy of magnolia dandruff in front of her house. In her bedroom window she wears only a tiara. Catullus elects a visit, after toggling his fingers to replay the message, her voice riding the answering machine, electronic music percolates in the background, "Yes, I'll be here.... Why can't you just call? You could have come over.... Okay, maybe it's good to go out.... I just have a lot of housework to do. Why was your voice so weird on my machine? Are you ever going to grow up...or is this high school forever?" Mahelly's voice ends, Catullus shaves, adjusts his mouth to a concave frown in the mirror.

Picking up his lazy corpse, his own extreme scent suggests (to himself) a haircut, O unkempt bard black hair grown over ears; the rest just jets forward, bangs drape toward thin eyebrows, grey eyes veiled briefly in sheath of tea fog

No more dumb words, fastening his breathing, tighter muscles, clenched fists, drawn drapes, locked doors, snow-stain memories thudding brick, concrete versus tailpipes, ventilation systems, telephone and cable wire

as heart palpitates, as oxygen affixes, as palms redirect movement and air barrels through nasal passageways, as purple veins rise to skin's surface (natural tattoos), as skin rotisserie-garbles across antique fillings and molars, bulbous fistfuls, mammary-mix, palmed aftershave or baked female sweat

this will be, Catullus thinks, *a caveman handling, a dearth in language, a shallow mutual fuck show*

it seems like I've been here recoiling
it seems like I've been here recoiling

in first person
in first person

moist May morning gurgles, fresh orgy of magnolia dandruff
moist May morning gurgles, fresh orgy of magnolia dandruff
moist May morning gurgles, fresh orgy of magnolia dandruff

and this is her song
and this is her song

I've been here recoiling I've been here recoiling I've been here
recoiling
it seems like
O it seems like

moist May morning gurgles,

Up the echoing stairwell of her house Catullus (is able to)
shed   clothing
Mahelly is reduced to temporary submissive rhetoric, via
narrative arch, stretching, exhaling
He arrows his mouth into her centre of attention
as outlined in countless napkin sketches,
Mahelly spits up his fingers, licks then wraps with banking precision
digits around dick, rubs her clit, nuzzles it,
"*identidem*," she says, mouth forming *m-sound*
fingers go deep, "put your tongue flat,"

[time lapse 14 minutes]

Mahelly pulls it out (of her) knapsack turnsswitch
turquoise, well-worn, joke-kisses it, hands it to Catullus
as she backs up, spreads herself, locks eyes on his
begins to pump, buzzing compromised by lipsswallow
swelling gritty motor moans *in out in* volume
after they play her pink circles close
after they play   pink   close

Catullus rises, shakes a box of windowsill couscous.
In front of the window he shakes the box of _____.
"No, seriously," Mahelly says with a flat snooze in her voice,
"what is couscous? Tell me what it is?"

On her tummy tensing bum muscles thunder
rain running unangular down house sides.
Nobody notices time dissolving into day.
Lodged lust swallows lovers whole.

Gives up on the couscous, tumbles back asleep
dreaming in argument tugs with an unnamed
actor as
Catullus tries manfully to intercept
insomnia, looks at curled form on futon
while one mind rehearses love's treacherous speech:
I want you I like you I need you, we really care about each other.

**(Blocking is required for much of this scene, for example, what is
Mahelly holding? What are these characters touching? Where is her hair, bits of it
in her mouth? Ponytail? Gummed in the next mission of trench war sex?)**

Precision, he cannot miss, Catullus with a burning thud building in his hand.
His blood races, charging coital reception to its most convincing channel.
He spanks harder each time, counting up to five. Fluting kiss looting, two hands
meeting in between two goldfish in a bathtub. He upends her sleep; her semicolon
mouth is slow to pronounce, "How long was I asleep for? Is that the right time?"
Paws for shirt, grabs shirt, an uneven ring of spit left on the pillowcase.
"I have to meet my sister for lunch. Want a lift home?"

Catullus runs his boxers up his legs,
nods his head affirmative
during these naked rituals,
where unlit thumbprints
pinch corporeal investigation,
rinsed in hot _____,
Catullus is the abject humiliant,
new questions how long it's been
since the last time—never says:
how many years / has it been / since
I ever / felt a body on my body/ crashing
orgasm / squeezed from me / lick / lift /lift off /
lunge /Jupiter, are you witness to this spiritual
contaminant / with herbs and minerals lascivious?

(Seriously, you need to block this scene. I understand Mahelly's got to
get out the door to meet her sister, but in how much of a hurry is she?
Does she bother to put on her underwear, for example? I want to know that.
And what colour is it, does it get twisted, does she look over at Catullus to see if he's
watching her get dressed, and does she roll her eyes, flutter them flirtatious, or trickle
a bit of tongue, laugh irresistibly or is she feeling insecure? To what, beyond the boxers,
is Catullus clinging during this rather forced epiphany that he obviously never had,
as it is totally implied that it is a "narrative projection"? Also, in one version isn't there
a line she uses about the size of her eyes when she's on ecstasy? Because they're
big to begin with, right? What? They've never done *E.* together.
No drugs, is that in his contract? Right, okay, I'm just going on what I'm reading,
or what I've seen in different drafts.)

Faith

well I guess it would be nice
downloading your body from a tiff,
a traumatic outfit,
tonight, my medium is the paper cut

early in the perennial wound
the reader is informed of
a reluctant collision with
an exhausted theme;

human drama
adjusts its jaw,
opens wide
hides itself from
purity

 a variation on, see also
"romantic locust,"
"thermal underwear trapped in baby blue sex"

              +

"parks smeared in karma"

OLDER

"Regret the solar system, then refocus. Change is a stranger.
He puts his hand on my body—all but a floral print thong between us.

I laugh, and wink, I fulfill my physical obligation like a vaccine or
mineral gaining speed, being studied in the camouflage of life.

When he leaves, I burn his business card and put my dress back over my head.
It's an honest exchange—monster.

My body is flawless, my mind is building itself for someone else.
This is economy, lower class."

MOLTEN EXCUSES

1.

"Seriously, Catullus, I shouldn't even be talking with you about
this. Was this before or after you spoke with her? I just got a phone
call from my little sister; I hope that you did honestly take care of
this. Because I hate this, because, I mean, how do I respond
to something like this when the role I'm forced to play is the
supportive friend? Like I said, I do truly hope you've taken care
of this. I'll play you Mahelly's message, here listen:

'Hey,
I think Catullus's feelings are hurt.
When I saw him yesterday. I do maybe like him a little.
But I don't like liking people.
I feel like I just want that security again or something.
It was hot with Rufus. But I don't know? It is hot with Catullus.
Sorry, details you don't want.

I suck. That is all.'"

2.

Not an apparition, something deliberate, eventually cruel.
Not a conclusion, drawn from some tinsel-drunk napkin
smear; a Cinderella—hopped up on disenchanting materials.

With subjective scorn, villain here has milked this anthem, jingle
and all, rendering it pitiless for all occasions. Until tattoo eclipses
skin, O how he will be fine, colliding apoplectic awareness
continuous sore igniting wounds silenced by gobbling vacancies,
chandelier's glow soldering tears of resolve,
his face, a thick tide flooding, heart drowning, no, *flossed* in blood.

3.

Time, space, present tense tightens flush on his closed mouth.
He squeezes plush pillow, hand burning, kisses a tidal wave, digests
a meteorite into molar, a molten excuse, hushed on inner leg, fostered
by touch, exploits ghost mouth soak your chops your soaked chops
he hears,
I want to hear your tongue...

Not an apparition, something deliberate, eventually cruel.

4.

Mahelly rehearses a scenario as she drives. Her hand creases the
page, which she props up on her knees, trying to aim it toward the
interior lighting:
"In the back of my spine I feel like a monster is inflating: I have to
destroy everything because this horrible energy washes over me,
overpowers more than me."

Thanks for Breaking Everything

Wishbone sling,
   I spread and bear details,
     Thursday, all night, until
      the bite is finished.
       Thursday never comes.
        The days don't have names anymore,
         just hangnails resembling flower petals.

       I'm not sorry. This love is a splinter, welted
       in hissing hornet tongues I cannot weather.

       I haven't strength for this,
       I, a jaundiced cobra, belly-up
       snickering fat in good meal delight—
                  my last.

       I am the mirror, the no one
       you have taught me the art of honesty
           in
       silhouette.
       Scold me with final sex.

       Let out hem of regret, kiss, fraying
       negligence.
       Underhanded grammar, dress that grabs
       at sweat, feel the second-person bomb explode,
       cathartic, supporting a quarry no barrel can hold.
       Outrun the pain variables, and antidote for this
       inappropriate lust.

No. 50 Revolting: a Conflict Variable (Unsuitable for Regret)

I have felt no earth
  growth growl
I have hurt no earth
  loathe lust
I have heard no earth
  froth foul
I have only seen
  urge weaned

O watch potent irreversible syllables
saliva broach regret necklace around
jugular
O washed up seven-inch words,
even in their most active of canons,
cannot celebrate the tear dick thief
of one great thud of love

in French *le baiser,*
in Italian *il bacio,*
in Latin *osculum,*
let's use *basia,*
kiss, soft Celtic word
from his native tongue,
the dud
      of compassion
    the rash of abandonment
    abject sprite
lacquered in carnally reddened, perfumed,
panting dementia, glad to have met you,
most stinging stingy
oar I use paddle raw

to a simple range of minor depth: *it is*
invincible knowledge renews amnesia
Let's pretend we never met, the dud
      declares.

Y Chromosome Y

creative control for the work weak
impotent werewolf howl captured
in a glass jar
past the fourteen-day return
period

chromosomeone's large blue eyes
lids tented with silver makeup
bedaubed in irreversible tears
muffled in red sweater lint
[dramatic pause]

the way the world pushes hands
across tables, bones grafted into
unsuitable grooves

I am bigger than blood or guns,
as friend as fungus lungs,

vilification comes in all sizes;
tamper with evolution,
craw back in Kafka cum shot
apprehension, defer your
demented academia

a swarm of foolscap coitus
a blizzard of dental   poses
migrate into sleep patterns
become a dirty   jpeg
ball cap nods,   jet-lag
eyeliner, first year newborn
stripper pups
consume cotton classroom

take nuts, notes, pills smelling
like cheap cake, pencil, lip gloss,
plastic snap ball-cap
vice, saucy lip tug, pen cap
bite, a thousand headshot
photocopied smears
all snug in cotton alibi.

Pain Variables (Group Rate)

Through the bedroom window, the fiery sphere slides benignly, tumour-like in the woollen clouds, stinging the lining of Mahelly's abandoned bikini bottoms. While you were gone, Catullus, your muse jumped ships and said, "Harder, don't stop," in morose Morse code, tapped out by Rufus in the discount honest night.

"We're not getting back together. Would you have preferred that I didn't tell you? It was just sex. It was bad. It wasn't like us. I didn't want to do this over the phone. I told you not to fall for me. Remember? Remember what I said? What did you think would happen? I wasn't leading you on. You broke all the rules, you called me sweetheart and baby, grabbed my hand, I didn't plan for this to happen. Are you thinking about me with other boys? No one ever treated me the way you treated me. I just wanted to be able to hug him again. I slept over. I loved the poem you wrote about me. I slept with him. Do you still believe we were meant to meet? People fall in love with me because of the way I look. You can't even look at me can you? We slept in the same bed. I feel like I'm not allowed to touch you anymore. I called you but you didn't answer. I was with him when you called. I don't want you to picture me with him. My phone was in another room. You care about people so deeply, it's nice. You should be careful."

PAIN VARIABLES (GROUP RATE)

The main thing here is to explain how the story of poems, kisses and fumbling dildos is unravelling at top speed down a spiral staircase smeared in sweat, cum, karma and baby powder, how some are playing parts, while some are just playing with themselves. The fact is, Catullus's agent is about to pull up in front of the house and present him with a brand new deal. Simultaneously, Mahelly is preparing to invite Catullus onto the back deck to join her for a cream soda and half-confess love and deceit, and Catullus has nearly completed his first poem in centuries, "Chills," which will be examined for any traces of his own gene; a gene that can only be passed on, it is believed, through the male Y chromosome.

The house is ghastly clean. Walls have been blasted in bleach as have the floors and countertops. Even the caramel-coloured drapes shine, the staircase bare of mail, newspapers, takeout bins and mucous-fossilized scarves.

For more information see Haplotype, Catullus.

JUVENTIUS FOR SALE

The wind and railroad tracks digest the campus simultaneously as Juventius scurries home with stationery and Popsicles. Despite the wind, Juventius has a smile on his face. The tracks he crosses divide the strip mall and the engineering building. As he strolls downwind, he notices the fragile relics of foot treads and sparse ice. *Soon*, thinks Juventius, *I will have a fresh start*. He wants to feel fear, but cannot detect it in his system, he feels strong, certain and without choice. To start with, the phone interview with the gym went well, really well. The manager said he could start in a week, but at one of their out-of-town locations. He agreed to that chance and promised to send the other office manager a resumé as soon as possible. That was his morning, restless at home, preparing a list of errands, stretching and taking out the recycling. He has special stamps, five of them. He has a box of envelopes. Tucked under an arm is a second-hand book on cover letter and resumé etiquette. Nearly home, Juventius witnesses a car hit a recycling box, it's carried under the grill for half a block. As the vehicle comes to a stop, Juventius dashes to the front of the car, noticing the box is caught under the license plate. "That's some wind," the driver says. Juventius feels good, nods and tosses the box onto a nearby lawn. He feels even better that he didn't dent any of his envelopes. The Herculaneum wind continues its theatre, Juventius will soon reach the house, dodging the moping Catullus to get down to work.

CHILLS

He poured his antique face on her
Final draft practice pout,

He watched her comb her long wet hair
It saddled every doubt

He vacuumed, he waxed,
Cleared his heart all bare,

A lifetime of regret it seemed,
Was biding on its heir

"At least we had these moments," he raised an empty glass,
"If everything was perfect, I wouldn't knead your ass."

So he did a moral inventory,
And mourned what he drew back.

CHILLS

In this house, we all share and challenge the mute reverb of slaughter-house love letters, leotards and perfumed arousals; like a wind of sand, you did not expect any of this enhanced envy,

dripping, digitally remastered in thick malt thuds made from nudging the rabid dog-eared menu; read each word anyway, four weeks, hoping for something sweet to crush against those stupid little perfect lips,

harsh, orbiting permanent in bravado red—O Mahelly, my tolerance for the parade trampling is infinite.

Week One

Round qualities hardened things; salivate salvation, coddle fascination, leap naked into mesh of slow-motion baby powder; constellating her soft suckable skin break up the stars into her mouth, feed her notorious love nutritious.

Week Two

The green-bottle sky goes wet-faced against the bedroom window as I tadpole-kiss the warm hearth of her behind...all morning.

Week Three

Running late for work, replenish parched flasks of hope with soft tongue pulls, donate eager sex grants; flash me on the banister, blanket angel, until I'm unemployed.

Week Four

Listening to Dino sing "On An Evening In Roma" on repeat again tonight. Drinking Merlot, making mussels. Miss her so much. Grab the genuine girl!

Found Text Messages

Pain variables found by Catullus on Mahelly's cellphone: 7

Come back! 2:48 PM September 30
Call me I'm alone now. 1:05 PM September 29
No wanna talk. 4:17 PM September 28
Things are bad. 1:15 PM September 28
What's wrong with me? 1:45 PM September 30
Working?   1:15 AM October 13
Is that an invitation?   6:34 PM October 14

Analysis: The above lexical arrangements provided a spine to the otherwise vague narrative Mahelly had been providing Catullus for the better part of the evening of October 1. Cold, calculated and sincere, Mahelly's willingness and Rufus's loneliness forged in the night as the melancholy bard prepped his chest with cough rub. Catullus had lent Mahelly a sweatshirt when she left his house on September 30. I can't say that I didn't see it coming, nor that my theory was without alternative ending. He would be betrayed, until he was removed from the sad constellation of lust.

The Catullus gene begins innocently enough with unnecessary staring, then splinters into its abject quest in the possessive unfaithful tense. As love shows early signs of failure, the Catullus gene inflames, amplifies and parades a drowning sense of panic. Some call it "sympathy conditioning." The final stages teeter on the brink of three main chambers: claustrophobia, self-destructurilization and, finally, the immolation of loss. Other side effects include: the universal souring that ushers in each new nervous millennium, and reconciliation failures, which rely heavily on numbered pain variables (*see next poem*). The more unstable the circumstance, the more deliberate and calculating the gene becomes. Like hate and love, its power will outlast its host: the loser after all.

The Loser After All

I seriously want to vomit tears and cry vomit.
anonymous pain variable (No. 69)

it was not surgery
it was not surges
it was wrought with urges
it was rot mergers

principle investor:
the loser after all

thermal denial
eye-duct drought
"God makes it easy to write about
treacherous
weasel-poking scabs of jealousy,"

the evening dimmed itself cheap and quick our
Catullus sat looking out the window into
exhausted man-made nothing,   cough syrup
bottle counter-clockwise turn, tap tap hot
lava bath, while   autofellatio failed to cramp
the loser after all

From the pain-variable Rolodex
        flip fleck rip wreck:

74 "You are hurting me, I feel trapped."
78 "Sex for you is physical, sensual, earthy, orgiastic,
        masculine."
92 "Having someone inside you weighs a lot."
54 "You're just jealous because it's *my* fantasy."
46 "I lay beside you and masturbated.
        I had to touch myself. I hate you."

Licked awful stomachs! quivering constellations of sperm
spiked vocabulary volcanic! cold sores gleamed and snapped
faulty! digestive cables cankered in turmoil! moaned
the loser after all

"I swear I hear someone else in this place," Catullus said,
his head damp in Juventius's lap, as entire molten nightmare
ignited for the ORIGINAL MOTION SICKNESS SOUNDTRACK

cued up cranial tissue weeping glistening cheat anecdote

doped up,
mouth mugged moist centre
a forecast of regret precipitation
testicles embalmed again not aging
                        knot ego

life is a mudslide, so
life is a mudslide, so
Catullus drank

The wine was menstrual in his mouth,
uncasually he prayed something was pregnant
"Listen to these words," he self-seizes,
"they express the furthest thing from our love."

145 "How did you get my postal code?"
a ballet of knives, ballot box stuffed with sore throats
and rage. **85** "You wasted my time." Hours of soup,
sleep, tea, then what? Figments of haunted joy touches,
long drawn-out dopey self-arousals failed to exorcise
collective pain cells crammed with content stomach
rusted in convertible ulcers, he craved pills trained to
invent sleep. **91** "We're not getting back together."
23 "You are a possessive unfaithful pervert."
97 "The floccinaucinihilipification is mutual."
57 "You square prehistoric fetishist."

sweet
self-loathed
oven-roasted
corporeal estate
drastic surgery
nostalgic gash
iodine-scented,
the loser after all

As if fresh from quarantine, Catullus
clenched his eyes, held his side—even
more curious than his physical pantomime
was how his own hunger seemed ornamental,
prearranged: three celery bites, four raisins,
a spoonful of mushroom soup

"Rufus again, Juventius! Rufus again! Did I tell
you this one? Even in the park, a mother and
daughter walked their dog, and the dog's name
was Rufus. I scalded myself in sick-day homeless
clown laughter. Juventius, I feel so sick."
        "Sleep on the couch with your puke bucket."
        "My stomach is killing me."
        "Rent is due, Rufus has moved out, he didn't leave a note did he?"

Juventius cooked a solo meal of edimami beans, Indian-style eggplant,
trout with capers and baked cornmeal bread while Catullus bombed himself,
aiming his arts-and-crafts disaster into licking fits shards of affection carried by
a common-cold housefly. He insisted to Juventius he heard the lopsided fly say:
1345 "parted ways, our love was dumb." **593** "I don't want to cry over all the
illusions of love
    I have to sacrifice myself to."

howlingly dedicated
an unfinished mobile of
perennial dearth,
never ceased to orbit
the loser after all.

FORMALDEHYDE OUT

spotcheck before Bithynia
spellcheck bartender Basia

hyphenate hemline
enablers loosen

lip-gloss prequels irrumo
rinsed in second-hand asthma

dance shrapnel enters
vital sign language

O gagged husbandwidth
silk napkin clutters arteries

plot likens
pulse thickens

iambics rest in sweat-pooled
gum lines of the recently fondled

shatter stain glass
with sample cackle

headstone typo
no room for heir

STORM ADVISORY

an endless ream of postcard stills will drop
from the insides of closed books, teeming
with domestic surveillance:
chores chortling with sighs, ample cooking,
laundry segregation discussing library fines

j a g g e d   expired pizza coupons
midnight collages of college girls

voicemail: "Why does everyone say you are dying out?
I feel like the future, lived backwards, black wolves
running like pixels, disturbed on the screen"

a dilated code
a benign pupil
a red ribbon
        of blood
once a month
once a millennium

you want to tie
kite strings,
bury them into
his chest hairs like
kitten,
kneading,
lift him out of memories,
not his.

No. 59

The participants have shipped out, invoiced and reformed, detached from temporary construction. Juventius has moved out, now gainfully employed as a personal trainer, Rufus has gone overseas, Mahelly just last Friday was offered (and accepted) a great job teaching at a private school. The night migraines into surrender for the poet stilted in unrehearsable pain. As Catullus walks away from his agent's car, envelope tight under his arm, his neck lowers as if heavy chains beg him down. He walks toward the villa, a man stands at the front door, waving him in like hot lunch. Catullus looks at the envelope marked "All the Gory Sadness Is Over / Curfew the Dead," raises his head, runs his hand through his short black uneven haircut. The man at the door points to the envelope with encouragement; all their fingers gesture with curiosity. Catullus enters. The door closes tight, seamless.

No. 60

"pixilated blur of blood-gush!
pixilated blur of blood-rush!

Catullus! Within an environment of
remote and abstract threat I have found
us a dead body of work from which to read,
from which to create a re-enactment, blow
for blow; 116 poems instructing us on fate,
plot, mood and tense
or we can start fresh

pixilated blur of blood-gush!
pixilated blur of blood-rush!"

ALL THE GORY SADNESS IS OVER
I told you we would howl

from this proximity it's not stalking
we share a large pint of malt Viagra
sipped through bendy straw
tofu or not we sparrow fast forever

all the cycles have sickened
all the gory sadness is over
we will heckle Jupiter all night
without science or scholars
knot the telescope
in our shadowed boxers
dripping dry

I have executed the congregation
finish your conjugations
meet me in
isolation chamber C
with the safeguard carpeting

spectre never
you a double you
me a double me
on my knees gregarious,
gargling laryngitis tea

evaluate like encourage
joy valve
resolve like revolver
release single, "Roll Over, Catullus"

life diced
lies diced

lice combed
tombs toned
shafts shackled

now that you've relived it
relieve it; release its
caustic imprint
all the gory sadness is over
all is known, everything is nouned

overdose on pain variables
creates verb recollection
debt absolved, love solvent
become solved

No one can truly say that he has been loved
as much as my darling Catullus
has been loved by me,
No faithfulness has ever been so great
in any bond of love as has been found
on my part in my love for you

THE END

ACKNOWLEDGEMENTS

Beth Follett, Emily Schultz, Alana Wilcox, Sam Hiyate, Michael
Turner, Kerry Segal, Geoffrey Pugen, rob mclennan, Janine Armin,
Michael Bryson, Shannon Sommerauer, Bret Hart, Ken Sparling,
Jennifer Mulligan, Tabitha Kane, Todd Swift, Rebecca Godfrey,
Mary Williamson, Ewan Whyte, Greg Lebelle, Sarah Reinhart,
J.R. Carpenter, Clayton Simon, Marty Spellerberg, Zab, Dave Harrison,
Scott Pardon and The Smiths. Special thanks to the Kliq: Jon Paul
Fiorentino, Ibi Kaslik, Andy Brown, Victoria Stanton, Alexis O'Hara
and Catherine Kidd.

I found Aubrey Burl's *Catullus: A Poet in the Rome of Julius Caesar*
(Carroll & Graf Publishers, New York, 2004) to be one of the most
sensitive and engaging resources on the poems and life of Catullus
that I have ever come across.

"Beta Love" was first published in *Canadian Literature*. "Curfew the
Dead" appeared in Switchback and was originally broadcast in 1999
on CIUT 89.5 HOWL FM in Toronto. Other portions of this book have
appeared in essay and fiction forms in *Lichen*, *Forget* and *Melange
Magazine*. An early version of "The Father Weeds" was published at
Todd Swift's *Nth Position*. "Despondence Course" was first published
in the anthology *Velvet Avalanche*. An early version of "Quadrantaria"
appeared as "Clodia," a broadside, with Ottawa's *above/ground press*.
Portions of "Storm Advisory" appeared in *Grimm Magazine*. Other
poems, including *Attis Shrugged*, were published in Hamilton's
Grey Borders.

ABOUT THE AUTHOR

Nathaniel G. Moore remains a literary construct(or) in Canadian
literature.